life
coach

C

brilliant

life
coach

second edition

10 inspirational steps
to transform your life

Annie Lionnet

Prentice Hall
is an imprint of

Harlow, England • London • New York • Boston • San Francisco • Toronto • Sydney • Singapore • Hong Kong
Tokyo • Seoul • Taipei • New Delhi • Cape Town • Madrid • Mexico City • Amsterdam • Munich • Paris • Milan

PEARSON EDUCATION LIMITED
Edinburgh Gate
Harlow CM20 2JE
Tel: +44 (0)1279 623623
Fax: +44 (0)1279 431059
Website: www.pearsoned.co.uk

First published in Great Britain in 2008
Second edition 2010

ISBN: 978-0-273-74322-4

British Library Cataloguing-in-Publication Data
A catalogue record for this book is available from the British Library

Library of Congress Cataloging-in-Publication Data
Lionnet, Annie.
  Brilliant life coach : 10 inspirational steps to transform your life
/ Annie Lionnet. -- 2nd ed.
    p. cm.
  ISBN 978-0-273-74322-4 (pbk.)
  1. Self-actualization (Psychology) 2. Personal coaching. I. Title.
II. Title: Brilliant lifecoach.
  BF637.S4L5655 2010
  158.1--dc22

                                              2010032821

The publisher would like to thank David Godwin Associates for permission to use Come to the Edge, *Selected Poems of Logue* (Logue, C. 1996)

10 9 8 7 6 5 4 3 2 1
14 13 12 11 10

Typeset in Plantin Regular 10/14pt by 3
Printed in Great Britain by Henry Ling Ltd, at the Dorset Press, Dorchester, Dorset

About the author

Annie Lionnet is a life transformation coach with many years' experience in the field of personal development. She brings her love of life and people, of science and spirituality to her unique coaching practice, working with both individual clients and groups. With her trademark warmth, she inspires and guides her clients to create – and live – their best lives. Her mission is to help others find the keys to self-empowerment that lie within, and thus live a life of joyful authenticity. Annie is the co-director of Affordable Life Coaching (www.affordablelifecoaching.org), an organisation that believes in the innate potential of people to live meaningful and fulfilled lives. You can read more about Annie at www.annielionnet.co.uk.

'Be careful what you water your dreams with. Water them with worry and fear and you will produce weeds that choke the life from your dream. Water them with optimism and solutions and you will cultivate success. Always be on the lookout for ways to turn a problem into an opportunity for success. Always be on the lookout for ways to nurture your dream.'

Lao-Tzu (6th century BC; founder of Taoism)

Contents

Acknowledgements

I would like to thank everyone who supported me in writing this book – friends, family and my editor Samantha Jackson. In particular a special thank you to fellow life coach, mentor and great friend Nina Grunfeld for your generosity, inspiration, expertise and constructive advice. I am also deeply grateful to all the teachers and mentors who have illuminated my path.

Foreword

Each human being has the potential to change, to transform their attitude, no matter how difficult the situation.

Dalai Lama

Imagine waking up every morning excited about the day ahead. Imagine knowing that no matter what the challenges you faced in your relationships, your work or your family, you would always find a way of operating from a place of acceptance and willingness to learn and grow from the experience. Imagine having enough self-confidence and belief in yourself and your worth to always be inspired and optimistic about your life and your future. Would you like to create that reality?

If you feel drawn to reading this book then you are almost certainly interested in making some positive changes and enhancing the quality of your life. *Brilliant Life Coach* provides you with a step-by-step approach to creating your ideal life. In the process, you become your own brilliant life coach, learning how to inspire and motivate yourself to become the very best you can be. Think of yourself as embarking on a journey and *Brilliant Life Coach* as a road map with a clear set of instructions on how to identify where you are in the here and now, where you want to be and how to get there. Throughout the book you will find several tools and strategies to equip you for the journey and help move you forwards. Each step of the way encourages you to explore more of who you are and galvanise you into action.

What is life coaching and what can it do for me?

Life coaching is a way of providing you with all the information and tools that you need for your success and personal development. Simple yet powerful guidelines and questions show you how to take charge of your life, transform your thinking and set and achieve goals. Life coaching supports and encourages you throughout the process in the same way as a sports coach coaches an athlete to perform at their optimum before and during a game. Most importantly, life coaching is about helping you to commit to your happiness and success and enjoy the process of self-transformation.

Specifically, life coaching helps you to:

- recognise that you have everything you need within you to live a fulfilled life
- discover your gifts and resources
- become the best version of yourself and live in the vision of how to create that
- make choices that affirm you
- live a more balanced life
- commit to yourself and take action
- feel confident about who you are and excited about your future
- set goals and find your purpose
- deal effectively with life's challenges
- move through resistance and be willing to change.

So if you're ready to turn your life around and become a happier, more confident and empowered you, turn the page and read on.

Introduction

Human beings are multifaceted creatures. Our identity is made up of the sum total of our history, our many traits as well as our values and beliefs. Each aspect of us reflects a different facet. There is the adult part of ourselves which is responsible and independent and the childlike part of us that can be afraid to grow fully into all of who we can be. There is the masculine side and the feminine side. The hard worker, the rebel, the parent, the caretaker, the hero and the victim can all co-exist within the same personality.

We are not always fully aware of these different aspects of ourselves and some remain hidden whilst others tend to dominate. Some of them may even conflict or oppose one another. When a person's different parts clash, such as the self that is fearful of change and the self that is adventurous, we can end up feeling stuck in our lives. One part of us wants change while the other is holding on to the status quo. How do we move through this impasse and take control of our lives? What do we need to do in order to become more integrated, fire on all cylinders and discover our power and passion? To answer these questions we need to understand what drives and motivates us.

Our basic human needs are simple. In order to physically survive we need food and shelter. But in order to thrive we need much, much more. We need to give and receive love. We need to believe in ourselves, to have strong self-esteem, and fill our lives with the things that give us joy. This sounds simple enough. So why is it that our quest to be happy so often ends in disappointment and disillusionment?

The secret to happiness

Whether we are aware of it or not, many of our expectations are unrealistic. That's because we believe that the answers lie outside of ourselves. Often our thinking goes something like this: 'If only I could find someone to love and take care of me, then I would be happy.' Or 'If only I could win the lottery, then I wouldn't have to worry about money.' But how would you feel if you knew that the secret of your happiness exists within you and you alone? Would you feel excited and empowered or fearful and sceptical? Would you leap at the chance of taking full responsibility for your own happiness and well-being or would you feel daunted at the prospect of being that creative and powerful?

You are unique

Each and every one of us is unique and possesses unlimited potential. In Eastern philosophy the term *dharma* describes our individual life pattern. For example, it is the *dharma* of an artistic person to create, an acorn to become an oak tree and a caterpillar to metamorphose into a butterfly. So how exactly do we blossom into the best version of ourselves, how do we create a life which reflects our highest potential?

Life purpose

Your life purpose is the reason you are on this planet. It is what you are here to accomplish and the gift that you bring. Your life purpose isn't necessarily defined by the job that you do, it's much more about finding and living:

● your essence
● your natural talents and abilities

- what fulfils you and makes you feel alive
- your wisdom.

Think of your life purpose as a path that gives you a powerful direction for your life. As you journey along this path the experience and the learning that you acquire will also contribute to your life purpose. When you live your life purpose you live your life by design rather than by accident.

Value yourself

Your mindset shapes your experience and creates your reality. Positive thoughts and affirmations create positive experiences and vice versa. Acknowledging what's special about you and valuing your unique aptitudes and abilities builds your confidence and empowers you. There's no place for false modesty in life coaching. When you value

> positive thoughts and affirmations create positive experiences

who and what you are, you attract people and experiences that enhance your life and reflect your positive self-image. Self-belief gives you energy, focus and confidence. The more aware you are of what is unique about you, the more creative you can be in designing your life. *Brilliant Life Coach* shows you how.

brilliant tip

The quality of your life is determined by the quality of your thoughts.

Infinite possibilities

There are no age limits on when you can change your life. Change is possible at any time. In quantum physics, the uncertainty principle states that the world exists in a state of pure potential and there is an infinite choice of possibilities. Any of these infinite possibilities can become reality with the right catalyst. When you decide to fulfil your potential and live your best life, you tap into and activate the many choices that are available to you.

Embrace change

Even if you are resistant to change – and most of us are at some stage in our lives – it's going to happen. This can feel unsettling to the part of us which finds security in stability. But when you invest too much in the status quo you are in danger of atrophying. The irony is that even when we are bored or unhappy with our lives, we may still continue to cling to the same partner, the same job, the same cramped space that we inhabit. There are many reasons for this and we aren't always aware of what motivates our behaviour. Sometimes it's simply a fear of the unknown. Or we may unwittingly have settled for the lives that we have, not daring to think that there could be so much more.

Rather than limit your choices and live in fear of what change will bring, you can learn to be the instigator of change and embrace what it has to offer. Perhaps it is not so much the unknown we should fear with all its potential for growth and self-discovery, but rather the known. In the known we stay where we are, in the unknown we become pioneers and adventurers creating new horizons for ourselves.

In honour of your unique self, it is essential to acknowledge the special qualities that make you the person you are. If you are unique, then you are also incomparable. What excites and inspires you may leave someone else cold. And yet so often we compare ourselves to others and find ourselves lacking. We fail to see our own gifts and talents and in the process deny all responsibility for our own progress and happiness. It takes courage to take a long hard look at yourself and fulfil your potential. But when you don't take control of your own life, you are in effect delegating this job to someone else. When you take charge of your life you become more self-reliant and less dependent on the opinions and expectations of

> it takes courage to take a long hard look at yourself and fulfil your potential

others. You take back your power and take full responsibility for what you want. You put yourself in a position where you can make decisions of your own choosing.

Explore your comfort zone

During the course of your life you will move through many different phases. At the beginning of each new phase you embark on a new path. Some of these paths are clearly indicated and you'll have no hesitation in taking the next step. But sometimes we are afraid to move forwards. We want some kind of guarantee before we risk any kind of change. Or we ignore the signs and choose to stay where we are. Even if we know that it's time for a change, we often flounder at each crossroads and find it difficult to make a decision. Determining which direction to go in can be a challenge. And choosing can seem daunting and even overwhelming and often requires courage and faith. So how do you become clear about which direction to go in? And even when you've decided on a course of action, how do you take the first step and move out of your comfort zone?

What is a comfort zone? It's wherever, however or whatever you have been and what you are used to. It's a combination of situations and circumstances that are familiar to you; your thinking patterns, your habits and daily routines and the people you spend time with. You'll know when your comfort zone is being impinged on when you react strongly to having to do something differently or being in a situation that is unfamiliar to you.

It's natural to want to have comfort and routine in our lives. It gives us a feeling of being in control and predictability and there are definite times in our lives when retreating into our comfort zone is our best move. After a long and demanding day it feels good to snuggle under the duvet and watch an old and much loved movie. The problem is that we end up trying to hold on to our comfort zone when change is inevitable – or required – and we resist new directions which are opening up for us. When we do this we sabotage our potential for a fuller and happier life. And we don't feel the passion we want to feel. Our lives become lacklustre.

Ask yourself how much energy you spend trying to stay in your comfort zone and protecting yourself from change in your life? It may be more than you realise because often our investment in maintaining the status quo is unconscious. For example, you may be sincere about your desire to grow into your full potential but not if it involves any big changes. You may have an unspoken contract with yourself which says: 'I am willing to become all of who I am as long as I don't have to look at my relationship, change my personal habits, re-evaluate my situation at work etc.'

Can you think of any ways in which your growth is conditional upon your life staying the same?

In order to move forwards you need to let yourself expand beyond the limits of your comfort zone and what is familiar to you. But before doing that it might be helpful to review your life to date. Are you happy with the choices you've made? How close are you to realising your dreams? Have you given up on them or are you still holding on to them? Reviewing your life can give you a sense of what is no longer working and help you identify what you would like to do next. Most importantly, it's an opportunity to think more creatively about how you

are you happy with the choices you've made?

can live your life more fully, find your life purpose and engage your passions.

Your heroic journey

When you decide to change your life you embark on an exciting adventure in which you discover what's really important to you and how remarkable you really are. Think of it as a heroic journey where you discover and develop resources, strengths and talents that you never even knew you had and achieve something of great importance to you. And in the process, you acquire a self-confidence and belief in yourself that is worth its weight in gold.

Each chapter of *Brilliant Life Coach* marks a new stage of your journey and will guide you through a series of steps to empower, inspire and motivate you to create the life of your dreams. You may find some chapters more thought-provoking than others. Take as long as you need and don't rush the process. It's your journey and you set the pace.

So, are you ready to move forwards and create your best life? All you have to do is make a commitment to taking the next step and your brilliant new life will begin to unfold.

CHAPTER 1

Prepare for your journey: how do you begin to transform your life?

Come to the edge
We might fall
Come to the edge
It's too high!
COME TO THE EDGE!
And they came
And we pushed
And they flew

Christopher Logue, Poet (b. 1926)

Take control

Have you ever thought that there may be more to life than you are currently experiencing? You may have a secret longing to leave your job and pursue a totally different career. Or get out of an unfulfilling relationship so that you are free to meet the partner of your dreams. Whatever is prompting your desire for greater happiness, something in you is ready for new experiences and possibilities. So why can changing our lives feel so challenging? Sometimes it's as simple as not knowing how to. But more often than not we feel unequal to the task of taking control and directing the course of our own lives.

When you doubt your ability to make decisions concerning your own well-being and happiness you fail to thrive and are left feeling dependent and powerless. Deep down you know that you are denying yourself and it doesn't feel good. In contrast, when you take full responsibility for your happiness and rise to your full stature, you assume authority over your own life. You become authentic and you are able to confidently, capably and joyfully steer the course of your own life.

brilliant definition

To be authentic is literally to be your own author – to discover your own intrinsic nature, abilities, and desires, and then find your own way of acting on them.

As you learn the skills and techniques of becoming your own life coach it will be your energy, determination, persistence and vision that moves you forwards. You will choose the goals that inspire and excite you and once you've realised your goals you will be entitled to take full credit for your wonderful achievements.

Where you are now

If you are happy in your life and feel that your circumstances allow you to be fully yourself on every level, then there may be little you wish to change. If you're not as happy as you could be, then you are probably feeling that there is more to life than you are currently experiencing. Whether it is inspiration or desperation that is prompting you to seek a more fulfilling life, before you make any changes it's important to acknowledge how you feel about your life right now.

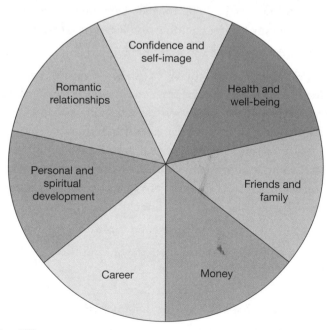

Circle of life

Aspects of life

The 'circle of life' is designed to help you get an overview of your life and how you feel about each aspect of it. Within each aspect of your circle of life there are a few key points to consider. You will have your own take on what each segment means to you, but here are a few pointers:

Confidence and self image:

● Which words you would use to describe yourself. Your list will probably have a mixture of positive and negative characteristics.

● What kind of impression do you make? How do you feel when you walk into a room? Can you ask for what you want?

Health and well-being:

● Exercise – are you getting enough or doing too much?
● Diet – are you eating healthily and listening to your body?
● Addictions – are you addicted to anything and if so, how are you dealing with it?
● Maintenance – do you regularly have a massage, dental and health checks?

Friends and family:

● How would you describe your relationship with your parents? Are they supportive of you or do you blame them for anything?
● Are you and your siblings on good terms?
● Do you enjoy your children or do you find them hard work?

Money:

● Abundance – how prosperous do you feel?
● Spending – do you live within or beyond your means?

- Generosity – do you enjoy sharing your money?
- Lack – are you afraid of financial scarcity?
- Debt – are you struggling to survive?

Career:

- Job satisfaction – do you enjoy your work?
- Salary – are you paid enough?
- Relationships – do you have good relationships at work?
- Performance – are you pleased with your level of success?
- Work environment – can you function at your best?
- Do you have aspirations that you long to fulfil?

Personal and spiritual development:

- Potential – are you committed to becoming the best you can be? If so, are you doing everything you can to make this happen?
- Purpose – have your found your purpose in the world?
- Religion – do you have one and if not, do you feel the absence of a religious framework to your life?
- Faith – do you believe in a power greater than yourself?
- Gratitude – are you aware of the blessings in your life?

Romantic relationships:

- Relationship patterns – are there recurring themes in your relationships?
- Commitment – are your desires a match with your partner's?
- Sexuality – are you comfortable with your sexuality?
- Sex – are you happy with your sex life?
- Self-love – do you love yourself? Do you feel worthy of love?

The areas where you have scored the lowest may be the areas that you choose to set goals around later in the book. As you

 **action**

On a scale of 1 to 10, ask yourself how satisfied you are with each area of your circle of life? Don't think too much about this, just put down what you feel intuitively.

commit to changing your life for the better, your circle of life will reflect that change as everything comes more into balance. Think of your circle of life as a compass, guiding you to a happier and more authentic you. You can revisit your circle of life at any point during the journey to see how you are progressing.

Be completely honest with yourself when you fill in your circle of life. This may be difficult at first because you may have been denying how you really feel about certain areas of your life. As you start thinking about yourself and your life with more clarity and awareness you will find it easier to evaluate your life.

Resist the temptation to feel despondent about any low scores you might have but rather see these as a spur to make this part of your life much happier and more fulfilling. You will naturally use higher or lower numbers depending on whether your tendency is to see the glass as half full or as half empty. What matters is that you are being true to yourself.

Create balance

Much as we love the idea of having every area of our lives harmonious and in perfect balance, the truth is that we are always in dynamic flux and needing to make adjustments. Having a more balanced life is a skill that can be developed, much like physical balance. How many of us can stand on one leg without wobbling? With intention and practice we can acquire greater equanimity and feel more in control of the way in which we live our lives.

Question your life

Being willing to question your life, even the things you are reluctant to change, shakes you out of your old way of being and opens you up to perspectives that you hadn't even considered before. When you get curious about your life you have the power to make it better. Your commitment to staying open and curious means you can start life afresh at any given moment. Zen Buddhism calls this beginner's mind, and it has a way of generating opportunities and creating possibilities that you don't see when you are entrenched in a fixed point of view.

 brilliant definition

The root of the word curious comes from the same Latin origin as the word cure, *curare*, which means to heal.

If you've ever wanted to move forwards but felt as if you were just spinning your wheels, unable to gain any momentum in your life, you'll know how frustrating that is. Being stuck in one place makes us lose heart and depletes our energy. We may feel a sense of despondency, failure or inadequacy. Looking at your current reality without any judgement or stories about how things should be or what's wrong with your partner or job will help you to see everything more clearly and is a much more empowering place to start from. The good news is that being at an impasse and adopting a more detached perspective free of judgement and negative commentary can provide an opportunity to ask some questions and take stock of where you are in the here and now. And from that vantage point, you are in a position to change your thinking and your life.

Extend your boundaries

If you are at an impasse it means that the map you have drawn of your life is out of date and it's time to redraw it. In the same way that once upon a time it was believed that the world was flat and that anyone who got too close to the edge would fall off, we often act as if there is a limit to how far we can go in our lives. If you want to extend the boundaries of what is possible, you first need to develop a new and more expansive perspective of your life. If your current beliefs are limiting your ability to move forwards, it's time to challenge what you believe to be true. You need to look at your life anew and break free of whatever is restricting you.

Take responsibility

When you take responsibility for your own happiness, you stop hoping and waiting for something – or someone – to change. You come to terms with the fact that your happiness depends on you. And you begin to learn the importance of valuing and championing yourself, discovering in the process a sense of new found confidence. You begin to see how empowering it is to stand in your own centre of gravity and to take care of yourself. And you discover that as you learn to value your own resources, you become increasingly self-motivated. You learn that for the most part, what you get out of life is directly proportionate to what you put in. You also learn that much of life is a self-fulfilling prophecy and that when you expect great things and are willing to go after them, you are more likely to achieve them.

> what you get out of life is directly proportionate to what you put in

Change your perspective

One of the most powerful changes you can make is to shift your perception and your experience from feeling unable to change to one of knowing it is possible. Whether you make sweeping changes or a simple shift in attitude, once you open up to new possibilities and commit to change, your eyes are open to new experiences and your life begins to look and feel quite different.

 **action**

A way to increase your perspectives is to assess each area of your circle of life by asking the question 'Where do I go next in my life?' and coming up with as many different answers as possible. For example, if you have a low score in your career segment, your answers might be: hand in my resignation, get a new job, retrain, take a six-month sabbatical, go abroad, start my own business.

Give yourself time to really get a sense of what the world looks like from each perspective and ask yourself which ones are the strongest/weakest/ the most challenging and why. As you engage in this line of questioning you begin to acquire a deeper understanding of the different possibilities that are open to you.

Much of the way you view yourself, and the world around you, is a result of all the messages and opinions that you've absorbed over the years. As you begin to question your beliefs about how you should behave, how you should look and what you should do for a living, you start to redefine who you really are underneath the layers of conditioning and begin to let go of the beliefs and values that mask the true you.

Believe in yourself

The way you think and feel about yourself has a much bigger impact on your life than you think. Your outlook colours your expectations of life. If you expect to succeed you will. If you believe in yourself and your abilities you'll have the confidence to make things happen.

brilliant tip

You attract the experiences that match your beliefs and expectations.

Positive self-belief

Think of a situation in your life when you knew you felt really good about yourself. Can you remember what a positive impact that had? Perhaps you felt confident about your ability to impress a prospective employer and as a result you performed well in the interview. Not surprisingly, you were offered the job.

This also works in reverse. Our worst fears are usually confirmed when we have negative expectations.

Negative self-belief

brilliant action

Use these 10 ways to develop positive self-belief:

1 Develop your innate resources and talents.

2 Value your uniqueness and don't compare yourself with others.

3 Support yourself and back your own decisions.

4 Commit to your own happiness.

5 Be true to yourself.

6 Acknowledge how far you've already come.

7 Adopt a positive mindset and monitor your self talk – are your thoughts supportive and affirming of you?

8 Always take action on your behalf.

9 Never give up on your hopes and dreams.

10 Trust that if you've done everything to make something happen and it doesn't materialise, it's because there's something even better for you.

Recognise your achievements

How many of us truly recognise our achievements? So often we dismiss them and focus on what we haven't achieved. Take the next few minutes to reflect on what you have achieved so far and then answer the questions in the 'brilliant action' box opposite. Notice how easy or difficult this is for you and how good you are at giving yourself credit.

Mirror, mirror ... Be true to yourself

If you feel that your life isn't your own, you could be assuming a borrowed identity. As you slowly let go of the false image you hold about yourself, being true to yourself becomes increasingly important. You stop living your life according to the

self-knowledge is power

brilliant action

What do you feel you have achieved so far? These can be big achievements like giving up smoking or getting a promotion to smaller achievements like finally clearing out the attic. Write down five examples here:

1

2

3

4

5

What else would you like to achieve?

expectations of others and set your own standards and values. The more you honour yourself the better equipped you are to accomplish your goals. Self-knowledge is power as it enables you to become the best and most authentic version of who you are.

Getting trapped in a negative self-belief can seriously limit your ability to live your life to the full. But how you see yourself isn't necessarily a true picture. Much of your self-image is determined by your early experiences in life. If you grew up being repeatedly told that you couldn't sing, or were clumsy or shy, the chances are you ended up believing it. We internalise these beliefs and undermine ourselves in the process. And because our outer lives are a reflection of our inner lives, we often attract people into our orbit who mirror our negative beliefs. This stops us from doing things that we might actually enjoy and even be good at. When you recognise how much more you are than the limited notion you have of yourself, you have taken the next step towards living a fuller and richer life.

Adopt the right mindset

Before you can embark on any kind of change, it's important to start by accepting who and where you are in the here and now.

 **brilliant** example

Moving from a negative to a positive belief

Anna's French teacher at school had repeatedly told her that she was hopeless at languages. As a result, Anna lost confidence and failed her French exam. Years later, Anna was given the opportunity of being posted to France for her work. This involved a promotion and a considerable increase in salary as well as a six-month intensive French course to get her up to speed before starting the job. Needless to say, Anna's negative self-belief about her ability to learn a language brought up a lot of fear and anxiety in her. But the job appealed to Anna and so she decided to have some life coaching to help her regain her confidence. After a few sessions, Anna had transformed her thinking and was feeling confident enough to go back into the classroom. She was amazed to discover that she really enjoyed learning French again and because her motivation was strong, she excelled in her studies. She has been living happily in France for two years and now she even dreams in French!

That isn't the same as being happy with the status quo. It simply means that you don't judge yourself. By accepting yourself as you are and the present moment as it is, you are in a far more powerful position to make a change because you're not in resistance or burdened by feelings of lack and inadequacy.

brilliant tip

You can respond positively or negatively to any situation. It's how you react to events, not the events themselves that determines your attitude. Successful people are not better people, but rather bigger people who have learnt not to allow circumstances to diminish them or affect the way they see themselves. Any challenge facing you is not as important as your attitude towards it, for that will determine your success or failure.

Tap into your potential

Science tells us that we are only using a small part of our brains. This suggests that we are capable of doing so much more and being so much more than we can even know. At the same time, it's important to recognise our limits. Not everyone has the potential to become a rocket scientist, a gifted teacher or a devoted parent. Equally, when we come to setting goals, you need to know that these goals are within your grasp and that you have set yourself realistic targets for achieving them. Each step that you take towards your goals provides you with a sense of achievement and a deeper appreciation of your capabilities. As you grow in confidence you may be surprised to discover that your sense of what is possible changes over time giving you greater scope and room to manoeuvre.

> when setting goals you need to know they are within your grasp

Know what supports you

When you have energy and drive in abundance you know that you are operating within your limits. This is not to say that you should not push yourself or work to extend the range of your capabilities. Your self-confidence increases when you stretch yourself and you find out what you are really made of. But first you need to recognise what nurtures and supports you and what depletes you. When you focus on what is nurturing and sup-porting you equip yourself for any challenge.

Give yourself credit

No matter how many relationships you have with people, your primary relationship in life is always with yourself. You are your one permanent companion throughout the amazing adventure that is your life. Think about the qualities and characteristics that you would value in a travelling companion. Are you those things to yourself? It's often difficult to acknowledge ourselves for everything that is valuable about us. Yet if we aren't in touch – or we are too modest to declare – our qualities and achievements we are unlikely to aspire to our full potential. To remind yourself of everything that there is to admire about yourself, try the following exercise.

Begin by listing at least five things that you like about yourself. This is not the time to hide your light under a bushel. If you are having trouble coming up with five items, you will know that this exercise can really benefit you. If you are still struggling with what to include on your list, think of what you like about your favourite people, because these traits are probably qualities that you possess too. It's much easier to see what is good or admirable in others. But what we admire in others is very often a projection of our unacknowledged self and the talents and qualities that we haven't yet owned.

What I like about myself is:

1

2

3

4

5

Every day for the next week, add something else that you like about yourself to the list. At the end of each day, read the list aloud. If you're feeling really bold, you can do this while looking in the mirror. At first your voice may lack conviction but keep going back over the list until you sound as if you are starting to believe in all your likeable qualities. Fully acknowledging what you admire in yourself changes your expectation about your life. And when you have a more positive expectation, the possibilities are endless.

 **brilliant** recap

Remember that in order to expect the very best of yourself, you need to appreciate all of who you are. And that involves transforming your thinking so that you have nothing less than total positive self-regard. Now that you have reviewed the key areas of your life and recognised the importance of making yourself a priority, you can begin to open yourself up to all there is to discover and celebrate about you.

brilliant task for the week

Consciously focus on doing things that you like about yourself and notice how this impacts on your thinking.

CHAPTER 2

Find out what you *really* want

Desire is the starting point of all achievement – not a hope, not a wish, but a keen pulsating desire which transcends everything.

Napoleon Hill (1883–1970; pioneer in the field of personal development)

M ost of us are seeking a life filled with joy, love, a feeling of security, creative self-expression, enjoyable and meaningful activities and self-esteem. The more of these aspects we have in our lives, the more fulfilled and happy we feel and the more we are able to realise our potential. Finding out what truly fulfils you is the first step to creating the life that you want.

Get clear about what you want

Do you know what you really want? You may have a clear idea of what you want to change or improve in your life, such as having greater prosperity, becoming more assertive or starting your own business. Sometimes we know what we want but for all kinds of reasons, we don't know how to make it happen or we never really get going with it. We find ourselves procrastinating, thinking of all kinds of reasons to put everything on hold, or getting discouraged along the way. If this is true for you, then the following chapters will show you how to move your dreams forward and manifest them in the world. If, however, you haven't yet identified what you really want, the following questions will help you clarify your desires. You may also want to take another look at your circle of life and remind yourself of the areas in which you scored the lowest. These are almost certainly the aspects of your life in which you would like to experience greater fulfilment.

Keep asking yourself what you want

What you want will inevitably change at different stages of your life – sometimes dramatically. So, it's important to periodically ask yourself what it is that you really want. If you neglect to question yourself about this you can easily end up following old patterns, getting what you've always got and never giving yourself the chance to decide what's best for you. Get into the habit of asking yourself what you really want, from deciding what to eat and who to spend time with to formulating your life goals.

get into the habit of asking yourself what you really want

 **brilliant** example

Know what you want and act on it

Alex had always been a city girl and loved the energy and stimulus of living in a busy metropolis. When she came to see me, she was still enjoying some aspects of her life but was complaining of feeling tired and stressed a lot of the time. Also, although she had always been very healthy, recently she had started getting debilitating headaches.

During our first coaching session, it emerged that she was ready for a complete change of lifestyle and no longer wanted to live in the city. She visited a friend of hers who lived in a town on the edge of some beautiful countryside and instantly knew that she wanted to move somewhere similar. Some of Alex's friends tried to dissuade her from making such a big change, fearing that she was making a mistake. But she had found what she really wanted and was determined to make it happen. She explored the possibility of working freelance and within six months, Alex had moved to her rural idyll and set up her own business. And she continues to thrive.

 **action**

Are you happy with what you've got in your life? Are you still trying to work out your true priorities so that you can decide what to focus on and what to let go of? What – if anything – is missing from your life? Is it:

- a romantic relationship or more passion in an existing relationship
- the excitement of a new adventure
- more money
- a successful career
- vibrant good health
- something else that you can't put your finger on?

Take time to consider your answers and think about what you would like to focus on and what you really want. In which areas of your life would you love to have more pleasure, meaning and success? Knowing the specific areas of life in which you would like to make a change and create a particular outcome is essential if you want to create your best life. However, when we shift in one area of our lives it automatically affects everything else and so we change our whole life for the better.

How do you think you'd feel if you had what you really wanted? What difference would it make to your life? As you muse on these questions, give yourself free rein to imagine having what you really want. Notice what feelings come up for you as you engage in this process. Do you feel excited or apprehensive? Or both? The feelings of excitement *and* apprehension aren't mutually exclusive. Allow yourself to have both and as you work through the book, your positive feelings will almost certainly become your dominant reality.

> give yourself free rein to imagine

Know your own mind

Much of the frustration that we often encounter in our lives comes from making too much compromise on who we are and what we want. If we are overly influenced by others we may be swayed in one direction or another, simply because we are not clear enough or rooted enough in our own conviction about what we want for ourselves. In order to live at our best we need to be clear about what we want, live in accordance with what we value and stand for what we believe in. To do that you need to know your own mind and act accordingly.

> **brilliant** tip
>
> When you become really clear about what you want, everything conspires to help you to achieve it and opportunities to fulfil your desires present themselves.

Become more self-aware

Knowing what we really want isn't always obvious to us. Sometimes we are reluctant or even afraid to identify our desires and aspirations as we may feel that they are out of our reach. Even when we do know what we want we can still lack confidence in our ability to create it. Becoming aware of what you truly desire and how to fulfil that desire involves getting to know yourself better. So, why is it important to become more self-aware? Because it's the only way in which you can fundamentally take control of your life. It's the first stage of the journey to creating the life that you really want.

> **brilliant** tip
>
> To live to your full potential, you must investigate what you really want out of life and why what you want is important to you.

What would you do differently?

What does your awareness of the here and now tell you about where you're heading in your life? If you continue in the same mindset and carry on doing the things that you're doing, will you be able to look back and see that you achieved what you wanted?

Psychologists have identified three fundamental qualities which define a fulfilling life: pleasure, meaning and engagement. When all three are present we naturally fulfil our potential and live purposeful and productive lives. Each of us will experience these important life-enhancing qualities in our own unique way. But, before you can do that, you need to know what's important to you and integrate that into your life. When you can properly define how to live on your own terms you will be in the best possible position to put necessary actions into place that will lead you to success.

Do you feel excited at the prospect of having what you want? If not, the chances are that all the advantages and benefits that come with a life that you design and create don't feel big or compelling enough yet. To know what you want and make successful changes, you need to know not only what matters to you but also why these things really matter.

brilliant action

To help you clarify your thoughts, take a look at the following questions:

- If you could have anything in life, what would it be?
- If you were living your ideal life, what would you be doing?
- What does success mean to you? Not to society or to your friends and family but what does it mean to *you*?
- What would be *your* greatest success in life?
- What single thing would make you truly happy?
- If you were to live your life again, knowing what you know now, what would you do differently?

What did you discover about yourself in answering those questions? Often and without realising it, we live our lives according to what we think we ought to do or what our partners, family, friends or even society think we should be doing, rather than focusing on what we would really like to be doing. The important thing for you to pay attention to right now is what *you* want and *why* you want these things.

brilliant action

Make a list of 10 things that give you a feeling of happiness and well-being. Some will be immediately apparent but others you may have forgotten, especially if they haven't been present in your life for a while.

1

2

3

4

5

6

7

8

9

10

Once you've listed the things that make you jump for joy, consider the following questions.

- Why do you enjoy doing these things?
- How does doing these things enhance your life?
- What's really important about doing these things in your life?

- How would you feel if you couldn't do these things?
- Which ones would you like to introduce more of into your life?

Write your own mission statement

When you know the answers to these questions, you will have a much clearer sense of what you would like to have more of in your life. You can then write a mission statement that can be used to make decisions on what is important to you, what you will choose to do, and what you will choose not to do. This is an important step in deciding on what you want and living in a way that is completely in line with what you value most in life.

Mission statements are used by companies and organisations to state their purpose. They act as a guide to the actions of the organisation, spell out its overall goal, provide a sense of direction and guide decision making. Your personal mission statement describes a clear intention for your life and it will help you to stay on track with what really matters to you. It's a way of capturing the essence of what makes you feel fully alive and gets to the heart of your true purpose. Finding out and committing to your mission statement gives you a powerful and inspiring direction for your life.

Take your time

Here's an example of a short mission statement:

I am always open to new opportunities and activities that help me to grow and learn. My goal is to enrich my life and the lives of all those around me.

Finding one statement that really rings true for you can take some time and you may need to peel back the layers until you arrive at something which reflects exactly what you most want for yourself. This isn't static and you may find that your mission statement evolves over time as you grow in stature and awareness. Keep your mission statement close to hand at all times. You can either commit it to memory and repeat it regularly, or write it down and make sure that you read it as often as you can. Always keep it concise because living by a mission statement that is short and to the point will facilitate every decision you make and reinforce your commitment to have what you really want.

keep your mission statement close to hand at all times

 **brilliant action**

Write your mission statement.

Give yourself credit

As you start looking at your life as it is in the here and now you may be tempted to focus on what others have that you do not have. This can bring up feelings of envy, resentment and frustration, all of which have the capacity to undermine your ability to focus on your goals and desires. When you focus on what you don't have it keeps you from recognising how far you've already come and what you've already achieved in your life. If you can avoid comparing yourself to others, you may find it easier to enjoy what you already have. As you begin the process of creating what you really want, remind yourself of what you have already earned and accomplished over the course of your lifetime and give yourself credit for it. This will help you to feel good about yourself right now. When you truly appreciate what is already good in your life you can start to build more of what you want and call up a sense of accomplishment at almost any time in almost any situation. Almost all of us have at least one area of our lives which we can justifiably feel proud of.

Focus on what's important

Following our hearts can be difficult when we lack confidence or allow others to tell us how we ought to live our lives. This can be disconcerting and interfere with our resolve. When you are confident and have faith in your capabilities, you'll be more inclined to disregard unsolicited advice and to focus instead on what's important to you. As you grow in self-confidence and self-belief you will feel encouraged to forge a life path that is as unique as you are. It may seem like stating the obvious, but it's important to remember that in order to create more of what you want in your life, you need to know what you want and really believe you can have it. The magical thing about authentic desire is that when you begin to respect it, listen to it, and experiment with following it, it will take you in the direction of the most wonderful life you can imagine.

 **tip**

When you get really clear and honest about what you want, everything conspires to help you get it.

Get unstuck

It's hard to feel excited about having what you want when you're feeling stuck. Each of us will experience being stuck differently. For some it's having a dream and not knowing how to realise it. For others, it's not having a dream and feeling empty. Or feeling responsible for everyone. Or trapped in an unfulfilling job. Or waiting for someone to come along and make everything alright. Feeling stuck usually means that you're only seeing your situation one way and you don't like what you see. However you get

> we can always find ways of getting unstuck

stuck it's important to recognise that even though we all get stuck from time to time, we can always find ways of getting unstuck.

 **brilliant** action

So, where are you feeling stuck right now? Take some time to consider the following questions:

1 Where do you feel in a rut?

2 Where do you feel a sense of obligation?

3 Where do you feel there's no choice?

4 What is exasperating you?

5 Where are you going through the motions?

6 What are you tolerating?

What can you do about it?

Just articulating and acknowledging the situation when you're feeling stuck is often enough to get things moving. Somehow things don't feel quite so big, quite so overwhelming, quite as daunting when you choose to address them.

So look at the situation head on. Turn it from stuckness into a challenge that you're willing to take on and change. The following questions will help to galvanise you. Make your answers as specific and detailed as you can.

● What would you do if you weren't afraid?

● What do you want?

● What would you love to happen?

● What would you love to create?

These questions are powerful when answered honestly because they create and clarify a direction and pathway from wherever you are to where you want to be.

Trust in your own ability

How many times have you known what you wanted but dismissed it out of hand convinced that you didn't have what it took to get it, that it wasn't somehow possible?

Invariably this reluctance to go after what we want is rooted in fear. Whatever it is that you're trying to achieve, keep asking yourself what you would do if you weren't afraid. There's a big difference from feeling the fear and doing it anyway and the freedom which comes from finding that place within yourself which trusts in your own ability to make something happen.

 **action**

Is there an area of your life where you've lost the plot and no longer know what you want anymore? Choose an area in which you'd like to have a breakthrough (e.g. work, relationships, family, money, self-esteem). Check your circle of life if you aren't sure which one to choose.

1   Ask yourself what would make you feel most alive in that particular area of your life. An easy way to do this is simply to notice your energy as you contemplate the question. You might want to do this exercise with someone you trust and have them ask you the question. Make sure you spend the most time focusing on what really ignites you and makes you feel alive.

2   Next, for each life area that you've chosen, complete the sentence, 'If I wasn't afraid I would …'.

Here are some relationship examples:

If I wasn't afraid I would:

- be more honest
- honour my need for space even if my partner wasn't entirely ok with it
- be more committed
- show how I really feel.

Think of as many examples as you can in your own life.

If I wasn't afraid I would:

1

2

3

4

5

---

brilliant example

Jamal had felt stuck in his life for a few years before he decided to have some coaching. When I first met him, his wife had just left him and he was at a very low ebb. He'd lost sight of what he really wanted and had lost a lot of confidence. I decided to ask him the following questions to help him open up.

1 If you could not fail, what would you do?

2 What's the easiest thing to do?

3 What's the boldest thing to do?

4 What would be the most fun thing to do?

5 What's the counter-intuitive thing to do?

6 What's the safest thing to do?

As Jamal thought about these questions, he began to realise how much he wanted to go back to Australia and open up a café on the beach. It had always been his dream but he'd given up on it when he moved to England. During the following sessions Jamal gradually built up his confidence and belief in himself and started planning on how he was going to do what he wanted to do. A year later I received an email from him with some photos of his new beachside café. He'd turned his feeling of stuckness into a challenge that he was willing to take on and change. And he created what he really wanted.

What will you do?

When we don't take action, the moment passes. And nothing changes. So what can you do? Keep focusing on what you really want and what that would look like. Get clear on what you'd like to be different. And define the next step you need to take to move towards having more of what you want in your life. It may not be a big thing, but it will be something. And that's what matters. Just the next step.

> define the next step you need to take

Get clear

Getting really clear and honest with yourself about what you want and what you'd most love to happen is the first step. Even if you don't think that it can or will happen at this stage, it's important to name whatever it is that you want no matter how outrageous, ridiculous or far fetched the possibility might seem right now.

If you catch yourself shying away from thinking about what you really want, remind yourself of how you have already achieved some of the things that you want. That you can have so much more. It's your call. Challenge yourself to take a risk in order to realise your dreams.

brilliant recap

Getting clear about what you really want is the first step to creating your best life. You'll know what's right for you when you feel a sense of excitement about the future and what your life will look like once you've achieved your desires.

 brilliant task for the week

Make a conscious effort to think about what you really want on a daily basis. Keep reminding yourself of what's important to you and take action.

CHAPTER 3

Create a positive mindset and overcome your fears

We are what we think. With our thoughts we make our world.

Buddha (*c.* 563–483 BC)

It's the thoughts that count

It may sound like an exaggerated claim that we have the power to be so much more that we are, go beyond our present circumstances and create a richer and more meaningful life. But is it? The new science has proven that our thoughts have an impact on our outer world. In fact, they literally create our reality and everything that we experience in our lives. The problem is that whether we realise it or not, most of our thought processes, attitudes, beliefs and personal perceptions are self-limiting. And when we don't challenge our thinking or our behaviour, our brain keeps firing in the same pattern combinations. As a result we keep recreating the same thoughts and experiences and we fail to recognise our incredible potential or see the infinite number of possibilities that are available to us. By thinking different thoughts, we can literally rewire our brain and change our minds about what is possible. When we focus on new ways of thinking, we activate new circuits in the brain and make new synaptic connections. The more we repeat a new thought, the more hardwired it becomes in our brain. We can literally change our minds. And when we do, we can change our lives.

Awareness is the key

Before you can change your mindset you need to become aware of your habitual thoughts and actions and recognise how they impact on your life. Most of our automatic thoughts and reactions are unconscious but once we recognise them and make them conscious they no longer go unnoticed. And once you become familiar with how you think and act, how you behave and what you say to yourself, you then have the choice to stop yourself from thinking in this way and learn a new, empowering *modus operandi.* The process of unlearning old habits and thought patterns and learning new ones takes time and practice but when you persist with this incredibly exciting endeavour, you create a new sense of self and break out of your comfort zone and the habit of repeating the same old, same old reality. And instead of the world dictating how you think, *you* create and control the way in which you experience the world. *You* decide how you want to think, act and feel.

Befriend fear

Venturing out of your comfort zone will inevitably have some fear attached to it. Even life changes which you choose to make, such as getting married, becoming a parent or changing careers can activate deep fears. It helps to remember that this type of fear gives you an opportunity to question whether you really want the new life these changes will bring. It also sensitises you to how unsettling any kind of change can be and how you are feeling about whatever part of yourself and your life you are leaving behind.

brilliant tip

The only effective way to deal with fear is to walk through it.

Fear has a way of throwing us off balance, making us feel uncertain and insecure. It holds us to ransom and prevents us from taking risks. If, however, you acknowledge your fear and accept it as an integral part of life and any new beginning, you are less likely to be discouraged by it. When you feel fear you are being alerted to the fact that you are at the edge of your comfort zone, poised on the threshold between the old and the new.

Whenever you face your fear, you overcome an inner obstacle that has previously held you back. And in surmounting that obstacle, the landscape changes both inside and out and you move into new territory. You may never exactly welcome fear but you can learn to accept it as part of any change. See your fear as an opportunity to discover your innate strengths and your ability to grow bigger than whatever it is that feels so daunting.

brilliant tip

When you tune in rather than give in to your fear, you can decide what your best course of action is.

Dare to shine

It seems perverse to think part of us is afraid of being totally fulfilled and successful. But so often we are afraid of becoming all that we can be, perhaps fearing that we haven't got what it takes, that we will fail or be unable to assume the responsibility that comes with creating the life of our dreams. Often we perceive our reluctance or resistance to moving forwards as an external obstacle standing between us and our desires. However apparent that may seem, in reality the only real barrier between you and your success is you. The barrier is composed of fears and doubts about your ability to take the starring role in your ideal life. Change your fearful thoughts and you will see yourself very differently. Success is a state of mind. Happiness is a state of mind. If you want to be successful, start thinking of yourself as successful. If you want

success is a state of mind

to be happy, start thinking happy thoughts. You are what you believe yourself to be.

Create a virtuous circle

The first step toward changing your life is to decide that you're ready and willing to commit to being the best you. That means believing your life is worth living to the full and that you're not willing to settle for second best. This commitment to yourself creates a virtuous circle – the more willing you are to be the best you can be, the more energised and inspired you will feel. This in turn leads to greater self-confidence in your ability to bring about change. Positive beliefs create positive experiences.

What's holding you back from living your best life?

Are you playing small?

You'll know you're playing small when:

- You feel unhappy with the status quo but don't do anything about it.
- You wish you could be like someone you admire but don't dare challenge yourself to fulfil your own potential.
- You are afraid to be yourself and be seen and so you hide behind a mask.
- You always defer to others because you don't trust your own instincts.
- You don't like your job but it pays the bills.
- You feel directionless.

Playing small is underpinned by a fear of being all of who you can be. When fear and self-doubt hold you back your life doesn't feel within your control and whatever you truly desire feels out of your reach. You may have even given up on wanting the best for yourself or not really know what that would look like.

Releasing thoughts of self-doubt creates an opening for optimism and excitement. Your world expands and you begin to see new possibilities. Whether you are aware of it or not, opportunities are always being presented to you but you can easily miss them if you are trapped in thoughts of doubt and uncertainty.

Make a list of five things that are holding you back. For example, you may stay in an unhappy relationship because you are afraid of being on your own, or you may want to find a more interesting job but lack confidence in your abilities. Be completely honest with yourself. Acknowledging these aspects is half the battle.

What's holding you back?

1

2

3

4

5

When you review your answers, notice what appears to be standing in your way. Are you being too hard on yourself? Perhaps your inner critic is telling you that you aren't good or deserving enough. Or are you blaming other people or factors outside of yourself? Remember that the obstacles we encounter in our lives are invariably rooted in our internal blockages. The conflicts and dilemmas you meet on the outside are a mirror reflecting back to you the beliefs and values that you hold. Some of these beliefs and values may be so embedded that you are not even aware of them. Whether you are aware of them or not, they shape your life and are instrumental in creating your reality. Once you've identified what these are, you can choose to change them.

brilliant definition

An inner critic is the voice inside that is undermining and critical of you. This voice often stems from the messages you received growing up.

Break the vicious cycle of negative thinking

We have literally thousands of thoughts a day and most of them are repetitive. Every time we repeat a thought we reinforce it and give it more power. These repetitive thoughts create grooves or neural pathways in our brains and we will continue to think along these same lines *ad infinitum* unless we change our thinking. In order to break out of a vicious cycle of negative thoughts you need to replace these with self-affirming and empowering thoughts until these become the norm or your default position. Remember that the limiting thoughts and beliefs that you hold are not always conscious. For example, you might tell yourself that you want to find a more interesting job but deep down you may believe that you're not talented or clever enough to make a career move. When a subconscious belief is at variance with a heartfelt desire it can sabotage the fulfilment of that desire. When you determine which of your beliefs are no longer serving you, you can consciously change them.

> the limiting thoughts and beliefs that you hold are not always conscious

Create your own list of thoughts that hold you back. Think about these for a while and consider how they might impact on your life. Create a new list of thoughts that move you forwards, changing each negative belief into a positive one. Notice how you feel when you transform your beliefs into empowering and uplifting statements.

Thoughts that hold you back	Thoughts that move your forwards
It's hard to change	Change is challenging and exciting
I'm too old/fixed in my ways to change	I can make changes whenever I choose
I am not deserving	I deserve the best
I feel powerless	I empower myself by taking responsibility for my life
I am a failure	I am a success
I'm not clever/attractive/qualified enough	I love and approve of myself
Life is unfair	I create my own reality
I am afraid to take a risk	I take leaps of faith
I can't say no	I can say no

Negative beliefs:	Positive beliefs:
1	1
2	2
3	3
4	4
5	5

Make empowering choices

Limiting thoughts and self-defeating habits keep you stuck in patterns that limit your experience of life. Once you become more aware of a negative thought, belief or pattern, you have the option of changing that belief and making choices that empower and validate you. With awareness comes choice and with choice, you gain the freedom to live your life more authentically (see the brilliant definition of authentic self on page 3). You can have thoughts that make you feel good or bad, expanded or contracted, optimistic or pessimistic. When you change your limiting thoughts you change your expectations. There's no longer a glass ceiling above you stunting your growth and your potential. Start thinking of yourself as being the best you can possibly be and that's what you will be.

Move from fear to freedom

When we're feeling blocked we are often at a loss as to how to overcome the obstacles we encounter. Situations that frighten us can cause us to feel paralysed and as a result the status quo remains static. We may feel impatient, anxious or depressed with the fact that nothing is happening, or frustrated that things aren't moving as quickly as we would like. In the same way as you can use positive thoughts to change your life for the better, when you're in the grip of a negative thought your mind will conjure up everything that might go wrong if you venture out of your comfort zone. When that happens, you grind to a halt or retreat to a place that is familiar.

Staying with the devil you know can feel very tempting when you are afraid. But playing safe doesn't allow you to discover your strengths and innate resources and grow into the incredible and unique person that you are. When you choose to confront your fears you begin the process of becoming a stronger and more powerful version of you. Move past what is holding you back and you've unlocked the secret of living the best life possible for you.

move past what is holding you back

Remove the blinkers

You bring yourself and your beliefs to every situation. If you have tried to move forwards but the way seems blocked, you are probably holding a belief that your future possibilities are limited. Holding limiting beliefs is like wearing blinkers. They narrow your vision. Remove the blinkers and you have a 360-degree perspective of your life. When you affirm to yourself that you have unlimited potential you dismantle the brick wall that has stood in your way. As you free your thinking from limitations, all the possibilities that were on the other side of the wall begin to emerge.

 **example**

Expand your horizons

Maggie was terrified of flying. When her friends went on holiday to exotic locations, she stayed behind. After a few years of feeling very annoyed with herself for missing out on some wonderful trips she decided to do something about it. In her life coaching sessions, she learnt to replace her negative beliefs about flying into positive ones. Her daily mantra became: 'When I fly I feel safe and calm.' She also visualised herself on her dream holiday, sipping a cool drink on a beautiful, tropical beach. Gradually her desire to be on her paradise island became more powerful than her fear of flying. A few weeks later Maggie was ready to face her demon. She booked a short flight within the UK and equipped with her positive beliefs and expectations, she confidently boarded the plane. She did hold her breath for a moment on take off but Maggie had grown bigger than her fear and it no longer had the power to control her.

Two months later she flew to the Caribbean and had the holiday of her dreams. She had literally and metaphorically expanded her horizons.

brilliant tip

You have the ability to control and change your thinking patterns and choose your life experiences.

brilliant tip

It is not the absence of fear but the courage to take action that determines success.

Cut your fears down to size

Fear isn't all bad and we can never totally eradicate it. Nor should we try as it can serve a useful purpose. The flight or fight response can be critical to our survival. Fear can motivate us to meet an urgent deadline by working harder or, in more dramatic circumstances, gives a mother the strength to lift a car when her child is trapped underneath it.

More often than not, however, fear prevents you from fulfilling your potential by closing you off to life-enhancing experiences. As you gear up to facing your fear, a barrage of negative thoughts and emotions can suddenly appear. Even when you muster the courage to walk through your fear you can still feel a sense of trepidation. Once you come out on the other side and find that you are in one piece, you'll discover that your fear has diminished and you are stronger.

brilliant tip

When you recognise that you're bigger than your problems, you'll gain the necessary courage to overcome anything.

It's important to cut your fears down to size and recognise that the amount of time you spend worrying severely inhibits your capacity to create and accomplish new goals. Walking through your fears means taking risks and requires both practice and patience. Initially it's best to set yourself small challenges. As you grow in confidence you'll want to set yourself higher targets.

Positive expectation

Maintaining an optimistic outlook is essential if you are to achieve anything. When you are able to trust, life's challenges become more manageable because you have a positive expectation of the outcome. Staying positive does not mean that you ignore the difficulties or pretend that everything is fine. Acknowledge what is happening and how you are feeling and direct your focus on the thoughts that will energise you and help you to find solutions.

Positive thinking dramatically increases your chances of success in everything you do. When you are confident that you are worthy and that whatever you want to achieve is within your grasp, you start to trust and think more creatively. You start imagining positive solutions and outcomes and letting go of thoughts related to giving up and failure. In fact these words cease to be in your vocabulary because you begin to see everything as a learning curve. You focus on what you want rather than what you don't have. And you also start appreciating what you already have.

focus on what you want rather than what you don't have

Make space for new insights

Moving from negative or limited thinking to positive thinking is simply a shift in perception. Nevertheless, it takes dedication and persistence to adopt a new mindset. Whenever a negative thought enters your mind, immediately replace it with a thought that makes you feel good. With practice you will automatically dismiss self-defeating thoughts and give your undivided attention to the beliefs that support and affirm you.

It's important to remember that you don't have to be constantly striving and putting effort into changing your mind. When you relax your mind you create a space for things to shift easily and naturally. Give yourself at least 10 minutes a day to switch off by doing something that involves no thought, such as going for a walk, meditating or even doing the ironing!

brilliant tip

Your life is the embodiment of how you think.

Think about a time in your life when you faced a fear and found a way of moving through it:

- Which personal qualities did you draw on?
- How did this make you feel?
- What did you learn about yourself in the process?

Acknowledge yourself for having coped so brilliantly in that situation.

Can you think of a minor fear that you could face and overcome in a similar way?

brilliant recap

Remember that your beliefs shape your life, either positively or negatively. It doesn't matter how long you have held a negative belief, you have the power to change it. And when you have the courage to become all of who you can be, your self-belief gives you the confidence to shine and inspire others.

brilliant task for the week

Focus on one or two positive beliefs that energise you and have the power to galvanise you into action. You are literally creating new neural pathways when you change your thoughts and erode old negative thinking. Notice the impact that these positive beliefs have on you.

CHAPTER 4

Be true to yourself

'Open your arms to change but don't let go of your values.'

Dalai Lama (b. 1935)

Know your values

Imagine doing what brings you the greatest joy, such as expressing your innate gifts and talents or being with the people you love. When you are feeling fulfilled in this way you are living according to what you most value. When you clarify your values you discover what is essential to you and what brings you the greatest fulfilment. Your values underpin your character and offer you valuable clues about what is really important to you. Knowing what these values are and making sure that you are aligned with them is essential for your self-confidence and integrity.

Values are intangible and are not something we do or have. Money, for example is not a value, although your attitude to it and what you do with it will say something about your values (e.g. security, peace of mind, freedom, generosity, pleasure). Your values are often very noticeable to others. For example, when you meet someone you can get a sense of their values by what they're wearing, how they interact with you, and the opinions and beliefs that they express.

Alongside your beliefs, your values shape the way you see yourself and the world. Feeling strongly or passionately about something will inevitably reflect one of your values. For example, if freedom is one of your values you will seek to incorporate this into your life and you may experience anger or resentment if it feels threatened. If you value honesty highly then telling the truth will be important to you and you are likely to be intolerant of anyone who is dishonest. Discovering and clarifying your values will support your decisions and actions. When you don't honour your values you feel inauthentic and this creates an internal tension. When you honour your values you feel fulfilled and in harmony with yourself. There's a sense of internal rightness.

Here is a list of words and phrases that illustrate values:

courage, decisiveness, honesty, independence, loyalty, reliability, openness, responsibility, self-discipline, dignity, generosity, modesty, humour, integrity, intimacy, tenacity, positivity, space, trust, tolerance, recognition, free spirit, inspiration, accomplishment, to be known, personal power, connection, collaboration, lightness, beauty, risk taking, growth, peace, partnership, romance, harmony, freedom, excellence, adventure, orderliness, joy, success, truthfulness.

Discover your values

Doing what is fulfilling to you means that you are living according to what you value most. When you clarify your values you discover what is essential to you and what brings you the greatest fulfilment. When we live our values we feel in tune with ourselves. When we don't, there is dissonance.

The easiest way to discover your values is to look at your own life. For example, if you wake up in the morning feeling great because you have nothing that you have to do and no particular plans, your values are likely to be space and freedom. If you love reaching out to people and forming a deep bond with them perhaps your values are connection and intimacy.

List ten of your values. If you can think of any more, add them to the list.

My values are:

1

2

3

4

5

6

7

8

9

10

You might want to prioritise your values and see which ones feel the most important to you. These will be your core values and describe what is truly essential to you in your life. Your values can change at different stages in your life. For example, independence and freedom may be two of your top values for many years but intimacy and connection may become more important values when you are ready for a relationship. Of course it is possible to combine all four values, so that you seek a relationship in which your desire to be independent is still honoured. You can also combine your values so, for example, honesty/truthfulness/integrity reflect the same essence.

Once you've listed your values, ask yourself what is important to you about each one. Does your life feel congruent with each of your values? Be careful not to judge yourself. You're simply finding out what really matters to you and whether your life reflects this. Choose one or two of your top

does your life feel congruent with each of your values?

values – the ones that you feel most strongly about – and think about how you can bring these into your life on a daily basis.

Use your values to make decisions

When you're clear about your values you can start to discover what you really want from your life. When it comes to making choices and taking decisions, your values are the litmus test for action. In other words, your values are instrumental in everything that you do. Before you commit to anything or take action, ask yourself:

● Will this action move me closer to honouring my values or further away?
● If I take this decision, what value will I have honoured?

True fulfilment

Making decisions that are based on your core values will always lead to increased fulfilment because there's no greater feeling of well-being than living the full expression of who you are. Honouring your values is inherently fulfilling but it can be challenging. We can sell out on our values if we are afraid of the consequences. For example, two of your core values may be adventure and independence but if you have a fear around not being able to make enough money you may settle for a humdrum and routine job and suppress your desire for autonomy and excitement. If trust is a core value for you and you are going through a particularly testing time and everything feels shaky and uncertain, it might feel difficult to live according to your value. When fear has the upper hand it's harder to express your values and you're more likely to opt for a mediocre life rather than a magnificent one. Your ability to stay congruent with your value despite the challenges gives you a sense of rightness and wholeness. You feel in harmony with who you are. You are being true to yourself.

definition

A core value is a value that determines what fundamentally motivates you in different areas of your life.

Recurring patterns

Have you noticed that you keep having the same kinds of experiences? The situation or the people involved may be different each time, but the pattern is essentially the same. You leave a job where you are unhappy and undervalued only to find yourself experiencing the same dissatisfaction in your next job. Or you fall in love with someone who is very different from your ex but after a while the same problems start to emerge. If you're wondering why the same situations and people keep showing up in your life ask yourself this question: 'What is the common denominator here?' And if you are being completely honest with yourself, you'll admit that it is you. Remember that you create your experiences based on how in tune you are with your values, beliefs and expectations. If you live in harmony with these your patterns will be ones that you are only too happy to repeat. If not, your recurring patterns will be at odds with what makes you happy.

> you create your experiences based on how in tune you are with your values

Think of a current situation in which you recognise you are repeating a pattern.

- Can you think of a value that you are not honouring?
- Can you think of a belief that would change this pattern?

Write down your thoughts and see if you are inspired to live your value more fully.

How could you start to do that? What action would you need to take?

 example

Honouring a core value

Daniel had been married and divorced twice. He blamed his ex wives for the failure of both marriages. He felt hurt and betrayed and vowed never to have another relationship. After a couple of years he met a woman he felt very attracted to but he was afraid to get hurt again. Daniel's attraction to Sarah created a conflict within him and after wrestling with this dilemma for a while he decided to have some life coaching.

Initially Daniel refused to take any responsibility for his relationship patterns and the break up of his marriages. In time, however, he began to uncover the subconscious beliefs which underpinned his unsuccessful relationships. His powerful and dominating mother had instilled a fear in him of being controlled by women. This meant that he wouldn't allow himself to get close to them or reveal his feelings. So he became remote and shut off and eventually they left him.

In stark contrast to Daniel's fear around being intimate were his core values – loyalty, honesty, courage and commitment. As he wasn't honouring any of these values in his relationships it was no wonder he was so unhappy and the outcome was always disastrous. Daniel slowly began to reconcile himself with his values and see how important it was for him to honour these in his relationships. He also worked hard to change his negative beliefs to ones that allowed him to be more trusting and open. He plucked up the courage to ask Sarah out and a few months later he reported that he had never been happier.

 tip

Our experiences tend to reflect what we believe about life.

To thine own self be true

It is a paradox that we should long for a happy and successful life and yet remain firmly entrenched in patterns and behaviours that result in quite the opposite. Being true to yourself is the key. Settle for anything less and you limit your potential for joy and fulfilment and create the same experience of limited happiness. Honour yourself and celebrate your uniqueness and you become the best version of you. Take up the challenge of growing fully into yourself and you have a formula for living happily ever after.

See challenges as opportunities

In the Chinese language the words 'crisis' and 'opportunity' are the same. This is a fascinating concept and suggests that every challenge you encounter contains a powerful opportunity to grow beyond your current mindset and circumstances. The greatest success stories are created by people who recognised a problem and turned it into an opportunity. You'll find that every situation, properly perceived, offers you an opportunity to delve deeper into your true nature and discover new aspects of yourself. In the process, you'll feel inspired and excited about your life and what lies ahead and motivated to live at the edge of your potential.

> every challenge you encounter contains a powerful opportunity to grow

brilliant tip

Your beliefs and values have the power to move you towards happiness and success.

Love your life

The path to fulfilment can be unfamiliar and challenging. Choosing to live our lives based on our values is not the way

most of us have been brought up. Many of us unwittingly settle
for what we believe is our lot. We often make choices based on
what others want, what is easiest and what would cause the least
disruption. Choosing a life that you love is a bold and sometimes
radical choice. And to do that you need to acknowledge your
value and worth and recognise the many possibilities that are
available to you.

Come into your power

When you are able to honour and believe in yourself, life's challenges become more manageable – even exciting. Your values
and positive beliefs provide you with a powerful context for your
life. They enable you to feel 100 per cent committed to yourself
and to take right action. They enable you to stand for who you
are and fulfil your highest potential knowing that you are powerful and effective in your world.

 **tip**

Your life is the embodiment of how you think.

 recap

Remember that when you align yourself with your values you
come into your power. You discover your true colours and become
vibrant and radiant. You make decisions which are based on what's
right for you and you no longer repeat patterns which limit your
happiness. Life will always challenge you, but when you are able
to see the opportunities in these challenges you have a winning
formula for fulfilment and success.

⟋ brilliant task for the week

Keep track of how much time you spend working, reading, with your family, doing things that nurture you, etc. When reading for pleasure, what kind of books or magazines do you choose? From this activity you can deduce what is most important to you. How could you integrate these into your life on a more regular basis?

CHAPTER 5

Find your spirit of adventure

'Life is either a daring adventure or nothing.'

Helen Keller (1880–1968; author and pioneer who altered our perception of the disabled and remapped the boundaries of sight and sense)

Would you like a life filled with passion, meaning and abundance? Anything is possible when you tap into your adventurous spirit and open yourself to how powerful and creative you really are. When you dare to be all you can be you unlock the life force within you. And that is when the true adventure of your life begins. You'll know you've unleashed your adventurous spirit when you wake up eager to face each day and you feel good about who you are.

Everything changes

Change is inevitable and everything in life is constantly moving. Witness the phases of the moon, the planets moving through the constellations and changes of the seasons. Even the cells in your body are changing at this very moment. Every one of us faces change at different stages of our lives. When we are totally open to new experiences, the prospect of change is exciting. When we are resistant to it change can feel disruptive and even frightening. A very powerful way to transform your fear of change into excitement is by reframing your approach.

Instead of thinking 'I am afraid of ...', confidently declare 'I am excited about ...'.

Here are a few examples:

I am afraid of leaving my job	I am excited about leaving my job
I am afraid of taking a risk	I am excited by the changes I am making
I am afraid of going it alone	I am excited about becoming independent

Think about what most frightens you about making changes in your life and write down your thoughts. You may only come up with one or two obvious examples at first, but there may be others in the background. Notice how these statements make you feel. Now shift perspectives and change what you are 'afraid of' to what you are 'excited by'. Is there a difference in your energy levels?

I am afraid of:	I am excited about:
1	1
2	2
3	3
4	4
5	5

From fear to excitement

When you reframe your perception in this way a whole new world opens up to you. You change the way you see your life and in the process you release yourself from being stuck with the same interpretation or expectation. You move from seeing the cup half empty to half full. Suddenly so much more is possible. A new pathway opens up that wasn't there before and you begin to see a way forward.

Be willing to try something new

Alice laughed: 'There's no use trying', she said. 'One can't believe in impossible things'. 'I daresay you haven't had much practice', said the Queen. 'When I was younger, I always did it for half an hour a day. Why, sometimes I believed as many as six impossible things before breakfast.'

Lewis Carroll, *Alice's Adventures in Wonderland*

 brilliant definition

Reframing is a way of acquiring another perspective by taking the original statement and interpreting it in a different way.

Just for the fun of it, see if you can think of some wonderful possibilities that you'd like to create in your life. These may seem like impossible dreams, but let your imagination run wild and really allow yourself to visualise and feel what it would be like if you could conjure these things up. Write whatever comes into your head and don't edit yourself. Your imagination is a powerful tool so let it have free rein. One of the greatest minds of the twentieth century, Albert Einstein, said that 'imagination is more powerful than knowledge'. It's not so much what you know, but rather what you are willing to imagine that will inspire you to live your best life.

Let your imagination explore different possibilities.

The first steps towards creating the life of your dreams lie in the power of your imagination. You need to visualise whatever you want. When you conjure up a picture in your mind, you're creating the mental blueprint for your new life. Your imagination will show you how to turn your possibilities into reality. Think of things not as they are but as you would like them to be. You owe it to yourself to live your dreams.

you owe it to yourself to live your dreams

When you're inspired you make inventive choices. Each choice creates your experience, so when you broaden your mental horizons your life becomes more expansive. Regardless of your current circumstances, being adventurous and making creative choices becomes an enjoyable process and your inventiveness sparks new solutions that wouldn't ordinarily occur to you.

Move from everyday thinking to inspired thinking. Use your imagination and look at things as they can be. You don't know what you can really do until you try. All you have to do is act on your dreams. Become the best version of you that you can imagine. If you imagine you can, you can.

brilliant tip

When you trust your inner guidance you will create the life you were meant to live. Trust in the voice that says 'you can do it'.

Think outside the box

In order to find your adventurous spirit you need to be curious about finding out more about yourself and discovering unknown possibilities. When you're curious you're open to considering different options. And this curiosity leads you to new places in yourself and expands your experience of life. You open up to new worlds and different points of view.

Nobody really wants to live an ordinary life. But without a vision or a dream to manifest, our lives can feel rather drab and meaningless. If you want an extraordinary life, you need to think outside the box and suspend your judgements about what you think is and isn't possible. In order to live a life that is truly the best it can be, you have to be willing to radically change your thinking, to question and to grow. You'll find your adventurous spirit when you start thinking like a pioneer and begin to feel excited about stretching yourself and discovering all of who you are. You'll become flexible, open and willing to let new experiences come to you.

Albert Einstein is also famously quoted as saying, 'No problem can be solved from the same consciousness that created it. We must learn to see the world anew.' In other words, we need to step outside our old paradigms in order to imagine greater possibilities and seek a bigger picture. One way to do this is to shift your perspective, expand your vision and dare to contemplate a bigger life.

Start experimenting

Your adventurous spirit is just waiting to be discovered. And it's easier to access than you think. Start experimenting by taking a different route to work. Do things that you wouldn't normally consider and challenge those limiting statements inside your head that appear to be a fact of life but aren't. Here are a few examples:

- It's not really possible to change.
- I've never been good at …
- I can't have an amazing life because I'm not amazing.

Keep reframing. Take a dance class, learn to sail, sculpt, sleep on the other side of the bed, talk to someone you have admired from afar. Push yourself out of your comfort zone and keep motivating yourself to venture into the unknown. If you feel any resistance or inertia at the prospect of exploring something new, have another look at the list of things that you're excited about. Dare to add some more. Follow your intuition. And trust that whatever you choose to do is right for you and that your life will be enriched with the excitement of trying something new.

your life will be enriched with the excitement of trying something new

 **tip**

All growth and accomplishment involves taking a risk.

 **example**

Dare to change

Anil had been a teacher for several years. Although he was good at his job he felt drained and exhausted most of the time. When he was at university his dream had been to become a writer and he had founded and edited a magazine. He spoke very animatedly about this time in his life. It was clear that he was passionate about writing and that this was his true vocation, in spite of the fact that he hadn't made it a priority in his working life. Over the years he had written quite a few short stories which he had never shown to anyone because he didn't have enough self-belief to get published. During the coaching sessions Anil began to see how his playing safe was draining and demoralising him. He connected with his passion again and realised how much he wanted to make a career of his writing. Enthused and excited, he decided to approach a publisher with some of his work. The publisher loved Anil's work and his first book came out a year later. Soon after that he started writing full time. Anil had found his adventurous spirit and dared to reconnect with his passion.

 **tip**

Adventurous people think like explorers. They discover new places, change jobs or careers and take up new hobbies.

Faith it 'til you make it

Opportunities can present themselves in mysterious guises or unexpected ways. When you adopt an adventurous spirit you act on these. At the very least you explore what comes your way because you know that new experiences stimulate and enrich you. Being adventurous means interviewing for that job even though you feel afraid of failing or breaking out of a stale relationship even if you are afraid of being on your own. When you connect with your adventurous spirit you feel upbeat and motivated to move forward, confident in your ability to pursue your goals. Your determination to achieve a particular outcome becomes a driving force and even obstacles can seem like minor hindrances.

Make a commitment

Until one is committed there is hesitancy, the chance to draw
back, always ineffectiveness. Concerning all acts of initiative (and
creation), there is one elementary truth the ignorance of which kills
countless ideas and splendid plans; that the moment one definitely
commits oneself, then Providence moves too. All sorts of things occur
to help one that would never otherwise have occurred. A whole
stream of events issues from the decision, raising in one's favour
all manner of unforeseen incidents and meetings and material
assistance, which no man could have dreamed would have come his
way. Whatever you can do, or dream you can, begin it. Boldness has
genius, power and magic in it. Begin it now.

Goethe

Have you reached the point where it has become more difficult to maintain the status quo than to risk something new? This is a powerful moment and can mark the point of change in your life. However, in order to move from one reality to another you need to be able to commit. When you are ambivalent about what you want, opportunities tend to fall through, relationships that you feel half-hearted about don't work out, and your dreams don't materialise. When you make the decision to go for what you want, you begin to find resources that you didn't even know existed. The minute you make a decision wholeheartedly, things start to fall into place and you are able to attract support for your plans. The more committed you are the more back-up you get – and often from unexpected sources. Trust your intuition when deciding who to share your dreams with. If you have a dream that is precious, you may decide to keep it to yourself until it is strong enough to stand up to possible scrutiny and scepticism.

> the more committed you are the more back-up you get

Although it's advisable to avoid confiding in anyone who might rain on your parade, sometimes a negative response serves to strengthen our resolve and our sense of what is right for us.

Make a decision

It's only when we truly decide that we are ready for a particular opportunity, that we deserve a great relationship, and that we have something of value to offer that we are empowered and motivated enough to explore our options. That may mean that we have to let go of our old lives in order to make room for the new life we are going to create. The simple but powerful act of making the decision to live your best life increases your confidence and trust in yourself to change your life in whatever way you feel will make you a happier person.

Take a risk

If you do what you have always done, you will get what you have always got. In other words, if everything stays the same, nothing changes. Erring on the side of caution gives us a feeling of security. But it can also prevent us from daring to take a risk and living a full life. Taking risks is part of what makes us feel alive. It makes life fun and reminds us that we can make changes at any moment. But if we're not feeling adventurous, risk can seem scary. We may have a built-in belief that if we strike out in a new direction we'll lose our way or even our identity. Or we may fear that we have too much to lose by instigating a change. If we indulge in catastrophic thinking, we might even imagine that something terrible might happen. This is because so often we identify with trying to survive rather than thrive.

The difference between living life to the full and living a life of quiet desperation is how often you take risks. Accept risk as a normal part of living. View risk as a part of the process of exploring your world. Acknowledge the lessons you learn with each chance you take and move on. If you're brave enough to risk, to temporarily live outside of your comfort zone for a short period of time, you're big enough to create the life of your dreams.

Take control and trust

Choosing to see your life as an unfolding adventure means accepting that you don't have total control over everything that happens to you. This requires an element of trust. This is a deeper trust than just expecting things to turn out the way you want them to. It's a trust that says that no matter what, you are committed to changing your life for the better. You have more control than you think. Remember that your attitude alone will determine the way you experience your life. Just having the courage of your convictions can bring about positive changes to your life and your world. When you acknowledge that you are in charge of your own happiness, you are able to make many more choices.

you have more control than you think

What would you do if you couldn't fail?

If you knew you couldn't fail you would be amazed at all the things you're capable of doing. You have the ability to do things you never dreamed possible. The more adventurous you are in your thinking, the more adept you become at doing things that would have felt daunting before. Begin the journey and move to the border of what is actually possible.

brilliant tip

Start by doing what's necessary, then do what's impossible, and suddenly you are doing the impossible.

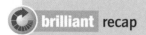

brilliant recap

When you find your adventurous spirit you can explore what it would be like if you could achieve everything you desired. Though this may seem a wild and romantic notion, giving your imagination free rein removes all the obstacles you would normally consider and clears the way to your true aspirations. You reframe your perspective and your life opens up. Let your imagination guide you to a truly fulfilling life.

brilliant task for the week

Start thinking about the areas of life you want to expand. You'll need to prioritise and select one or two that feel most pressing. Think of ways in which you can become more adventurous in these areas and commit to exploring different possibilities. Remember, if you can conjure it up in your imagination you can create it.

CHAPTER 6

Find your true talents and create your goals

'Go confidently in the direction of your dreams. Live the life you've imagined.'

Henry David Thoreau (1817–62; author, poet and philosopher)

Whatever journey you are embarking on, it will inevitably involve a goal. When you set goals you chart a course so that at some point in the future you and your dreams will meet. So where do you start? Before you decide on your first goal you will need to:

- be inspired
- know what you love to do and are naturally good at
- listen to your intuition
- know what you are committed to
- be confident in your choices.

Be inspired

We all know how it feels to be inspired. When we come from a place of inspiration we're lifted to a higher level of perception and so much more seems possible. We feel animated and motivated to explore our potential and follow our dreams. Not only that, but when we are inspired we are more likely to follow its cues and confidently act on our hunches. We dare to make far-reaching changes because we are operating from a place of greater trust.

We are all inspired by different things so our challenge is to discover what our own sources of inspiration are. Ask yourself: 'What am I naturally drawn to, fascinated by, curious about and energised by?' If you already know what inspires and uplifts you, the next step is to bring inspiration into your life on a regular basis. If you aren't sure what inspires you, or if it has changed, give yourself some time to think about it. When was the last time you felt a spark of your imagination? Or when was the last time you acted on an impulse that felt totally right? If you don't feel inspired, you are likely to lack energy and drive. When you feel inspired you feel uplifted and your energy dramatically increases. You connect with what ignites you and makes you feel vibrant and alive and you can start bringing that into your life.

 **brilliant** action

Ways to be inspired:

1   Immerse yourself in beauty – spend time in nature or in a beautiful place.
2   Do something that creates inner peace like yoga, t'ai chi or meditation.
3   Stand barefoot on a beach and enjoy the expansive horizon.
4   Absorb yourself in doing something you love.
5   Have flowers in your home and on your desk at work.
6   Listen to your intuition.
7   Focus on your dreams.
8   Do something you've never done before.
9   Pretend that you only have one day to live. What do you have a burning desire to do?
10 Tell someone special how much you love them.

Write a list of five things that inspire you.

Get excited about everything that you find inspirational and commit to being inspired on a regular basis. Keep adding to your list.

I am inspired by:

1

2

3

4

5

brilliant tip

Commit to bringing more of what inspires you into your life.
Inspiration isn't a single event; it's a daily activity.

Do what you love

Doing what you love and loving what you do can seem like a
luxury. But in truth, you can't succeed in any endeavour that
you don't like. If you don't love what you're doing, don't do it.
Instead, aim for something that really engages your qualities and
your talents and that you'd be happy spending all day doing.
Real success consists of finding the
joy and passion in everything you
do. If you're just going through the
motions in your life, admit to it and
vow to make a change. Ask yourself:

> if you don't love what
> you're doing, don't
> do it

- What am I going to do to become the best version of me?
- How am I going to bridge the gap which exists between
  where I am now and where I want to be?

What do you enjoy doing?

So how do you discover what you love, what you're brilliant at, what makes you happy and brings joy into your life? Instead of looking outside yourself start by looking inside at what excites and energises you.

Make a list of 10 things that give you pleasure, for example, listening to uplifting music, spending time with your loved ones, entertaining, having a massage, going to the theatre, curling up with a good book, being with children, writing your journal, being creative, giving to others …

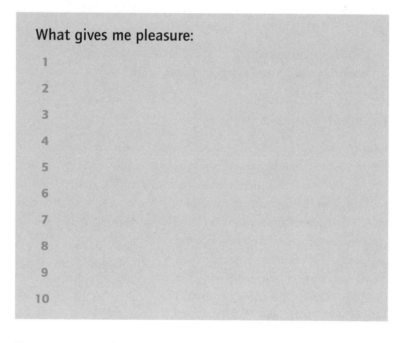

What gives me pleasure:

1
2
3
4
5
6
7
8
9
10

You may not realise it, but the things that you love doing often indicate your gifts and natural abilities. It is important to discover the gifts that you may not be using because they are an integral part of who you are. When you are working to your strengths and doing what you love, new dimensions open up in you and your life takes on a new direction.

Discover what comes naturally

Often we are too modest or doubtful about what we are naturally good at. But if we can't acknowledge and express our skills and abilities we can't become the best we can be. Ask yourself what it is that you do best. If you genuinely don't feel that you know, think about what you enjoyed doing as a child. What were you happiest doing and always wanted to do? What positive feedback did your teachers give you? What do your friends and family remember you enjoying when you were growing up?

Gather as many clues as possible. See this as a treasure hunt which will lead you to your true gifts and talents.

What I loved doing when I was growing up:	What I most loved about it:
1	1
2	2
3	3
4	4
5	5

Keep adding to the list of things and enjoy the process of acknowledging yourself in this way.

Listen to your intuition

Your intuition speaks to you through your feelings and your gut instincts. It's not something you can explain logically. You can tune into your intuition when you still your mental chatter and switch from the rational, linear left-brain thinking to the more creative right-brain thinking. When you listen to your intuition you find out what you really want. This may contradict what you think you should be doing. You'll know that you're listening to your intuition when:

- you are clear about what you want
- you 'just know' that you are on the right path even if it doesn't look as if you're going in the right direction
- your decision 'feels' right
- you feel a flutter of excitement in your stomach
- you feel relaxed and happy about your decision no matter what anyone else thinks.

Be aware of when you suddenly feel inspired to do something, no matter how unrealistic it might seem. You might wish you could paint a portrait of someone you love, or join VSO and work abroad. Listen to these urges because they may well be pointing you in the direction of your passion and what you love.

See the bigger picture

Feeling inspired to paint a portrait doesn't necessarily mean that you are meant to become a fine artist, although that may well be the case. At the very least you might want to take up painting as a hobby. However, there may be other ways in which you can express your creative impulse, such as choosing paint colours and home furnishings to transform your house. If you love doing this, you might even consider interior decorating as a career path. Don't limit your options. See the bigger picture. Think laterally. Be curious and find out what really turns you on.

don't limit your options

Daily practice

When you've found what you enjoy doing it's important to bring this into your life on a daily basis. This will build your confidence in your abilities and your desire to fulfil your potential. For example, if you wish you could write a novel, start by keeping a journal and make a space for this in your day – maybe last thing at night or first thing in the morning.

 **example**

Doing what you love

Anna was a natural agony aunt. From her teenage years her friends had come to her with their problems and she would know intuitively how to support, uplift and encourage them. Anna never considered how these natural talents could be used in the workplace and as she was good at numbers, she trained to be an accountant. After a few years she began to feel that she was on a treadmill at work. Apart from paying the bills, her job offered her very little else. In her life coaching sessions Anna listed all the things that she loved doing and it was obvious that she was passionate about helping people. After a brainstorming session to see how she could use her talents, she set herself a goal to become a counsellor and enrolled on a part-time counselling course which she could fit into her working life.

After two years, Anna handed in her notice and became a full-time counsellor. She had found and was living her true vocation.

What are you committed to?

When you're inspired to make any kind of change you need to have a goal. But before you ask yourself what your goal is, it's important to pose the deeper question of what you're committed to. Your goal is the visible outcome; your commitment is the inner desire that creates your goal. For example, if you are committed to becoming a successful photographer, your goal might be to have an exhibition of your photographs in a well-known gallery. Knowing what you are committed to will help you to set your goals.

The importance of having a goal

As you map out your goals you are stating your intention to achieve something important to you. Goals enable you to focus and move forwards. They need to feel compelling so that you are strongly drawn to manifesting them. In the pursuit of a goal, you grow in strength and stature by facing the inevitable challenges along the way. Each time you do this, you become more confident and self-reliant. No matter how big or small your goals are the process is always the same. First you need to know what you intend to happen. To discover your intention ask yourself this question: 'What is my ultimate goal and what steps can I take to get there?'

> goals enable you to focus and move forwards

Action steps to your goal

Goals can feel like a big undertaking and it's easy to associate goal setting with New Year's resolutions – something you have a good intention about doing but which you give up on sooner or later. A goal needs a plan to transform it into reality and your best plan of action is to break your goal into manageable steps as this will build your confidence in achieving it. Instead of only seeing how high the mountain is your first step is to focus on reaching base camp. Your ultimate goal is still to reach the mountain peak, but it now feels a much more manageable achievement.

For example, if your ultimate goal is to find a new career you might want to break this down into the following action steps:

brilliant action

1 Re-evaluate your skills and talents and what you love doing.

2 Talk to an expert or a good friend about your aspirations.

3 Explore your options by looking into retraining.

Trust yourself

When you set an intention and choose a goal to work towards, you don't always know how you're going to achieve it. So before you decide on the first step you need to remain open to the possibility that you can achieve something without having all the answers. When you are able to trust in this way, you can focus on your intended outcome without getting bogged down on how it will come to fruition. Trusting your own abilities to navigate from where you are to where you want to be builds increment-ally as you move towards your goal.

brilliant tip

Take concrete steps towards what you want and be open to both opportunities and challenges when they appear.

Be positive

Make your plans with positive expectation. The more inspired you are the bigger your goals. When you know that you are following your true path, you feel confident that your goals are realistic and attainable and this propels you forward. However, too rigid a plan can be counter-productive. It's also important to leave room for unexpected developments that might require a re-evaluation of your goal. You can take a different path and still know you are headed in the right direction.

too rigid a plan can be counter-productive

Make your goals real

When you set your goals you need to state them in the present tense, as if they were already real. For example: 'I have the job of my dreams' and not 'I would like the job of my dreams' or 'One day I will have the job of my dreams'. This may sound odd at first but your subconscious mind works best when your goals are positive and in the present tense. You also give your goal more power when you have a target date. A journey has a beginning and an end and an estimated time of arrival. This can be flexible but it's important to give yourself a timeframe to achieve your goal.

 **tip**

The first essential ingredient of success is to know what you want and believe you can have it.

Define your goal

When you choose your goals they need to be SMART – specific, measurable, action-orientated (what will you actually do?), realistic and timed. It's no good having a vague goal, such as 'be successful'. You must know what you need to achieve in order to be successful. For example, if being more successful means a career change you need to ask:

S – What specific steps will I need to take to change careers?
M – How will I measure my progress?
A – What action do I need to take to find the very best job for me?
R – How will I know that my goal is within my reach?
T – How long will it take to reach my goal?

Formulate your goal

Have another look at all the areas in your circle of life (see page 4) and choose which area(s) you would like to set a goal in. Remember that your criteria for choosing a goal is that you feel inspired and energised at the prospect of achieving it. If your excitement is tinged with a bit of fear don't be put off. This simply means that you are challenging yourself to move out of your comfort zone.

brilliant tip

Remember to write your goals in the present tense. For example:

Goal: 'I have a fulfilling and exciting career and I am valued and respected by my boss and my colleagues.'

This goal has a defined destination as you are visualising yourself in a job that fulfils you and matches your talents and abilities. Next decide on your target date. When will you reach your goal – in two months, six months or longer? Remember to create some action steps so that you can measure your progress and see how you are working towards your outcome. Measuring your progress reassures you that you are on track and heading towards your destination. Put a timeframe on your action steps. When are you going to start doing your research? When are you going to hand in your notice? Imposing some deadlines on your action steps keeps you focused.

What tangible results will there be when you've succeeded at each of them? Write down how you will know when each goal is completed. How will your life have changed when you achieve your goal? How will you feel? Let this be real for you. The more consciously you choose what you want in your life the more power you have to make it happen. Acknowledge your

affirm how good you are at making things happen

Goal 1:	Target date:
Goal 2:	Target date:
Goal 3:	Target date:

Goal 1 action steps:

1

2

3

Goal 2 action steps:

1

2

3

Goal 3 action steps:

1

2

3

progress as you work towards your goal. Affirm how good you are at making things happen. Be creative and flexible. If you feel you need to come up with some new ideas or new solutions, have a brainstorming session with someone who is supportive of your goal. This will help you to generate more options and discover the resources that you can bring to making your goal happen.

Feel good

Keep in mind that your life is an eventful and exciting journey. Feel good about reminding yourself of all the benefits you will reap in the process of achieving your goal. Picture yourself enjoying the benefits. Be optimistic. Expect miracles. See your wishes coming true. Acquire an attitude of positive expectation and it will keep you motivated. Congratulate yourself on having committed to your new life. Make this a daily practice.

Pace yourself

So often we want to reach our destination without experiencing the journey. We can run out of patience or even hope if it takes longer than we anticipate to achieve our goal. Each step of the way is a potentially valuable experience if you choose to see it that way. Everyone who has succeeded in reaching their goal did this by taking one step, and then added a second, third and on until they reached their destination. Trust that each step is taking you closer to your goal and believe unconditionally in your ability to manifest your desire.

Develop new strengths

Often our motivation is strong when we first set goals. We feel galvanised by the prospect of creating a new dimension to our lives. Some goals and dreams come to fruition relatively easily. Others are more of a marathon and require a tremendous amount of effort and self-confidence. And self-confidence is often something we feel we lack. It's easy to misinterpret our lack of confidence about making a change as an indication that we aren't ready. But in actual fact your lack of confidence is more to do with venturing into the unknown. You never gain real confidence in your ability to do something until you actually do it. Remember that difficulties and challenges will build your confidence, develop your inner resources and connect you with strengths that you didn't know existed.

You will build your confidence when you:

- take action
- set goals small enough that you can achieve them
- always expect the best

- learn something new
- move out of your comfort zone and feel more expansive
- celebrate each time you tick off an action step
- believe that your dreams can come true
- spend time with someone who believes in you
- don't give up on yourself
- do what you love.

Of course the times when everything goes smoothly are essential otherwise life would feel constantly challenging. But you really find out what you are capable of when you overcome difficulties in the pursuit of your goals. Your goals keep you in touch with what is worth working towards, and if necessary fighting for. And in the process you build momentum by strengthening the courage of your convictions and having something to look forward to. Your self-esteem expands, and your commitment to your goals grows stronger for having been tested. When you discover that you are confident and resourceful enough to overcome the obstacles in your path, you come into your power. Keep visualising your goal and focus on your intended next step. Your goals move you in the direction of your dreams.

> your goals move you in the direction of your dreams

Stretch yourself

Challenges are an inherent part of any new direction. You may meet them at the outset or further down the line. Believing in your goal and your ability to overcome any potential setbacks keeps you building momentum and moving forwards in the pursuit of your goals. Setting goals focuses your attention on what you want to create in your life. Without goals there is no achievement. As you set your goals it's important to redraw the boundaries of what you believe is possible. Your goals need to feel within your reach but at the same time somewhat of a stretch. By taking the risk of believing that more is possible for your life, you open yourself to greater possibilities. Feeling excited about your future is a clear indication that you're ready to set your goals.

Life enhancing choices

We make choices all the time. Some are life-changing choices and others are small, day-to-day ones. The choices that you make have a direct impact on the quality of your journey and the success of your goals. So how do you know if your choices are supporting your goals? Your choices need to be based on who you are, what makes you happy and what you need in order to thrive physically, emotionally, mentally and spiritually. These choices need to reflect your values and what makes you feel whole and good about yourself. To check whether your choices are enabling you to be happier and more fulfilled and to reach your goals, ask yourself:

● How does this choice make me feel about myself?
● How much better will my life be as a result of this choice?

When you are confident in your choices your goal feels irresistible and compelling and you keep taking steps towards it. Each step becomes an achievement that you can celebrate. And each achievement builds your confidence in the path you have chosen. You don't have to wait until you have achieved your goal. Even the smallest achievement is an indication of the positive choices that you have made and worthy of your praise.

 **tip**

When you praise yourself for how you are progressing you acknowledge the validity of your choices.

You'll know that you're making the right choices when:

● You feel a thrill every time you think about achieving your goal.

● You wake up with a sense of excitement.

● You see synchronicity everywhere in your life. Articles that you read, programmes you catch on TV and the radio, things that people say to you all confirm that you're doing the right thing. The signs are everywhere and they are all pointing you in the same direction.

● You have more energy than usual and a strong feeling of resolve.

● You feel impatient and raring to go, determined to become the best version of you.

● You feel in flow.

brilliant tip

Enjoying your life is a choice.

Your support team

You can also build confidence in your choices asking for support from the people whom you admire and respect. Their energy and encouragement will propel you forward. Sharing your hopes and dreams with people who you know will support you empowers your aspirations and helps to make them more real. Ask them to be there for you and to tell you, 'You can do it', 'You're incredible', 'Of course you're going to achieve your goal', whenever you need reassurance. Don't underestimate the power of getting the right support. Your resolve is nurtured and strengthened when you have others behind you. Having a support team of people who believe in you is the essential back-up you need to keep you believing in the choices you have made and to encourage you if you have a crisis of confidence. If you don't know someone who can make a difference to your success, you'll almost certainly know someone who does. You'll be surprised at how willing people are to give their support and share their knowledge and expertise. Think about how pleased – and perhaps flattered – you would be if someone approached you in this way.

your resolve is nurtured and strengthened when you have others behind you

Make a list of supportive friends, potential mentors, family members, colleagues or authority figures who can help you work towards your goal. When you approach them, be specific about your intended outcome and ask for help giving examples. For example:

- I'd like a new relationship and I'm thinking of joining an internet dating service. Do you know of any that are particularly good?
- I'm thinking of giving up my job and finding a different career. Will you help me to brainstorm some ideas?

brilliant example

Mihaela had always lived in a big city and done well-paid but not very fulfilling jobs. In her free time she made beautiful quilts and had sold a few to friends. Her big dream was to move to Ireland and make her quilts full time but she didn't know anyone who had done anything similar and she had no contacts in that part of the world. Mihaela shared her vision with her support team and one of them put her in touch with Claire, a friend of a friend who ran a textile business in southern Ireland. Mihaela plucked up the courage to contact her and a few months later they met. Mihaela loved the small village where Claire lived as it was full of artists and artisans and exactly the kind of environment she was looking for. Claire introduced Mihaela to some key people and within a year Mihaela had moved to Ireland and started her own very successful quilt-making cottage industry.

brilliant recap

When you discover your true talents and abilities, you grow in self-confidence and you feel inspired to set goals that will enable you to be the best you can be. There are many strategies that can help you to achieve your goals. Setting measurable goals and target dates gives you a clear and focused way of manifesting your desires and helps you to keep on track.

 brilliant task for the week

Pick one of your sources of inspiration and make it an even bigger part of your daily life. Notice how this helps to uplift and energise you in the pursuit of the goals you have chosen.

CHAPTER 7

How to make the *right* choice

Until we are free
to think for ourselves
our dreams are not free
to unfold.

Nancy Kline

The power of choice

Every day you make choices that empower you, enhance your energy and self-belief or that deplete and undermine you. From deciding what to think, choosing how to talk to yourself and others, your life is filled with endless options that lead in one direction or another. The choices that we make on a daily basis, no matter how trivial they seem, contribute to the quality of our lives and to what we experience. They either move us towards a better balance or they move us away. When we make healthy choices we honour ourselves. In fact, self-honouring is one of the most fundamental keys to creating a happy and fulfilling life which truly reflects our desires and aspirations.

So, how can you determine whether or not you are making choices that honour you? All self-honouring choices make you feel good about yourself and will tend to feel empowering; they will give you a sense of authenticity as well as a sense of balance and ease. When you make the right choice, you automatically feel good about it, excited, compelled, uplifted, energised and expanded.

Self-sabotage

Deep down we almost always know what is best for us in our lives, from the relationships that we create to the food that we eat. And yet, it is often difficult to make the right choices for ourselves. We may go on spending time with people who drain us or choose to eat fast-food over a healthy, nutritious meal. Often we have no idea why we continue to go against our better instincts but when we do, there is invariably a deep-seated part of us that does not want to make positive and empowering choices. And when this happens we are essentially self-sabotaging.

Self-sabotage happens unconsciously, which is why it's so difficult to see that we are doing it. On a rational level we may know our best course of action, but when we are in the grip of our internal saboteur we aren't able to follow it. Even when we have taken a conscious decision to make changes and move forwards, we can still find ourselves holding back, questioning or doubting whether we really have made the right choice for ourselves. This moment of hesitation can often be prompted by an insistent commentary in our head which threatens to squash or undermine our desires and aspirations.

> self-sabotage happens unconsciously

Confront your inner saboteur

One of the things that can keep you feeling trapped in a life that doesn't reflect your true nature and aspirations is the tendency to see problems instead of possibilities when faced with a choice. Often our greatest barrier to making healthy choices involves confronting and challenging the part of us that fears change and wants to stay small and preserve the status quo. This part of us is often at the root of our capacity to self-sabotage and is responsible for the way in which we hesitate, doubt or criticise ourselves, hold back and even shoot ourselves in the foot. Our inner saboteur is afraid of what will happen if we grow, take risks, make empowering choices and become all of who we can be, and often has its roots in all the shoulds, shouldn'ts, musts/oughts, etc. we have absorbed growing up.

What messages did you receive when younger?

Think for a moment about how you were brought up and educated. Were you encouraged to try new things and not worry about failing? Were you praised and supported and told that you could do anything that you wanted and that it doesn't matter what people think. Or were you warned to be careful, not hurt yourself or show off. Perhaps you were even told that you'd never make anything of yourself. The messages that we receive when growing up can have a lasting effect. And if these were negative, we have to find ways of undoing them if we want to have the courage of our convictions and the confidence to make the best choices.

brilliant tip

We know we're making the right choice when it feels exciting, energising, engaging and compelling.

Outside influences

Many of our choices are not really our own but are suggested to us from outside influences. We may truly believe that it is we who have made the decision but in reality we have actually conformed to the expectation of others. Having the confidence to make your own choices can be challenging when you are being swayed by the opinions of others or under the influence of your internal saboteur. It can weaken your resolve and leave you feeling confused and conflicted. Sometimes we realise that we are going against our own desires but whether we are conscious of this or not, when we hand our power over to others, it is usually driven by fear of disapproval, isolation and even abandonment and this feels like a direct threat to our 'comfort zone'.

Align your choices with your values

Our internal saboteur is the part of us that doesn't want to rock the boat, even if we're unhappy with our lives. When that part of us is in charge we essentially disregard our values and when that happens, the choices we make don't reflect our authentic selves. Honouring your values inevitably brings true fulfilment. When your choices are consistent with your stated values and your integrity, you automatically trust in yourself and this builds self-esteem, which leads to confidence, self-reliance and self-motivation. And the authenticity of your choices leads to a successful outcome. Each time you are faced with a choice, remind yourself of the values that you listed in Chapter 4 and check that you are honouring them.

> our internal saboteur doesn't want to rock the boat

What are you choosing?

We often question our ability to change our lives. We may be able to *imagine* living our ideal life but we don't always think that it's realistic to expect it. As a result, we lower our expectations to protect ourselves from feeling disappointed. For example, we may resign ourselves to the fact that having a great job which engages all of our skills and pays well is a big ask and should not be expected. So we choose to stay in a less than satisfying career even though we aren't happy. When we're not happy with our lives we rarely see this as something we've chosen. But on some level, we *are* choosing whatever the situation is that we find ourselves in, albeit unconsciously. Making a conscious choice to change our lives for the better gives us the power and motivation to live our lives in accordance with what brings us the greatest fulfilment.

 **action**

Focus on one particular aspect of your life in which you would like to make a choice, such as career, relationships or health and ask yourself the following questions. You might want to take another look at your circle of life to help you decide.

● What are you choosing for yourself in this area?

● Are you happy with the status quo?

● Do you have what you really want?

● What do you want more of?

● What do you enjoy about this aspect of your life and what do you dislike?

● What would be your ideal scenario?

Finding greater fulfilment may not mean, for example, choosing to change jobs or looking for a partner – it may mean changing your attitude or behaviour so that your life becomes more rewarding and enjoyable.

Weigh up the pros and cons

The capacity to make positive choices is essential for your healthy psychological functioning. And the choices that you make throughout your life shape the quality of the life that you have. Every decision has a potential upside and downside and making choices can mean giving up one path to pursue another. When the upside is more clear-cut it's usually easier to decide. When it is a close choice, it is more challenging. In that case, it is helpful to compare the benefits and risks of making a particular choice by writing a list of the pros and cons to give you a clearer sense of what's right for you.

Pros	Cons
1	1
2	2
3	3
4	4
5	5

We often hold back from making a choice when:

- we find it hard to take the initiative
- we find it challenging to commit
- we don't want to give anything up
- we are waiting for others or fate to make the decision for us
- we are afraid that someone will be hurt by our decision
- we believe there is only one right decision and we are frightened of getting it wrong
- we find beginnings or endings difficult
- we don't give ourselves permission to make independent decisions
- we don't want to take responsibility for ourselves.

If you still feel some hesitancy, review the reasons why you may be procrastinating. Check in with your intuition and see what it's telling you. Sometimes there is a good reason why it's not the right time to make a decision, in which case we have to wait until it feels right. If, however, there is no good reason why you shouldn't go ahead and choose, check and see whether your inner saboteur is throwing a spanner in the works. And decide that you are not going to let your fear stop you from making the best choices.

brilliant action

State the desired outcome of your choice, e.g. I want a job that engages all of my skills and abilities and that pays well.

1 Decide on a scale of 1–10 how compelling it feels to achieve your desired outcome.

2 What does it mean to *you* to achieve your desired outcome?

3 List all of the possible alternative choices.

4 Identify which choice best matches your desired outcome and write it down. Notice how you feel about this choice. Are you excited, enthused and energised? Do these feelings outweigh any apprehension you might be experiencing?

5 Explore any potential downside there might be to this choice. In comparing these consequences, is this decision a more positive or negative choice?

6 If it's a positive, enlivening and compelling choice, what action are you going to take?

Choose for yourself

Some of us find it easier to make decisions than others. If this is not our strong suit, we may develop strategies that invite others to decide for us, for example by putting off a decision until someone makes it for us. Another tactic is to ask advice when we already know the answer or seek reassurance in another way. If you recognise these traits, give yourself permission to think about what *you* really want and only ask for advice when you genuinely don't know the answer. Sometimes it's helpful to run your decisions by others but unless you are required to do so, you may want to keep your own counsel, at least until you are completely sure about your commitment to your chosen path.

> give yourself permission to think about what *you* really want

Expand your range of options

Have you ever stayed in a relationship or a friendship even though you've known that it wasn't right for you? It makes us feel safe and secure to stay within the world that we know. But equally, we may feel a strong desire to expand our horizons. The more we explore other options, the more insight we gain into what we like and what's right for us and discover more about ourselves in the process.

Develop a creative approach

One way of helping you become more adept at generating options is by becoming more creative in your thinking. Your right brain is responsible for creative and flexible thinking. Research shows that when your right brain is more frequently and fully engaged, you can come up with all sorts of innovative approaches to solving problems. Your left brain is designed for rational and analytical thinking and has the ability to evaluate situations and come up with a considered judgement. Both sides of the brain need to be actively engaged in order to make the best choices.

You might hold a limiting belief that you're not creative but in reality everyone is. You can harness your innate creativity to develop a more open mindset and change the way that you view your options. Becoming more creative can be as simple as interrupting some of the patterns that keep you stuck in old grooves, as we have seen in Chapter 3. Other ways to get your creativity going are listed below. Incorporate as many of these ideas as you can into your every-day life. When you decide that you are going to approach your options in a creative way you'll discover all kinds of possibilities that you'd never thought of before.

Here are some ideas to stimulate your creativity:

- Become more playful and discover your inner child.
- Read a book on a topic that you wouldn't normally be interested in.
- Discover different kinds of music to listen to.
- Change your routine, try a new food, buy a different newspaper, try on different styles of clothes.

Spend 10 minutes every week, thinking about ideas like this that you can try out and notice what happens. Be playful and experiment.

Have a strong intent

You're much more likely to make the right choices when you have a strong intention about what you want and express it as a desire statement. Remember that these statements are much more powerful when stated in the present tense. For example, if you want to get really fit and feel more energised your desire statement might be: 'I enjoy perfect health and radiate vitality and well-being.'

You will have many options for achieving this outcome, such as changing your diet, taking more exercise, taking up yoga or meditation, etc. Deciding which options you're going to take will strengthen your desire statement so that it becomes a tangible goal to achieve.

brilliant action

Think about the choice(s) that you want to make in your life and write your desire statement in the present tense. You don't have to limit yourself to one statement – write as many as you feel inspired to.

1

2

3

4

5

Remember to keep a positive mindset when you express your desires. Give yourself permission to accept that almost anything is really possible for you if you're willing to work on yourself and develop your resources. For each of the desire statements you have, think about all the different ways to get there.

Choose the best fit

Options invariably have upsides and downsides. When you think of your options, what feels safe, scary, difficult, risky, or exciting for you? What impact does each of your options have on your goals and aspirations? What factors do you need to take into account when considering your options?

When it comes to making a decision, you need to choose the option that's going to be the best fit for you in your present circumstances. Check your options against your intuition to see which path is right for you and ask yourself the following questions:

● Which option is the most compelling for me?

● Can I really see myself achieving my goal, despite any fears and doubts I may currently have?

● What, if anything, am I resisting?

- Is there an option that I'm discounting because of fears, doubts and concerns that I have about myself and my abilities?
- Is this resistance coming from my inner saboteur or from a gut feeling?
- What are the potential consequences of my preferred option in all the different areas of my life?
- Is my preferred option in line with my values?

Give yourself plenty of time to consider these questions and write down your answers. Is there anything else that you need to work on to move forwards on the option you are choosing?

What are the consequences?

Sometimes when we make a choice we realise that there are undesirable consequences in other areas of our lives. If you feel that is true for you, you may need to remind yourself of your core values and what is really impor- tant to you in order to galvanise your decision. It's vital to be really honest with yourself about the con- sequences of your preferred option.

> it's vital to be really honest with yourself

Your awareness of what you are doing – and why – will keep you focused and committed to your best course of action.

Get support

Once you know what your best options are you might decide that you need some support to make a definitive choice. It can be helpful to talk to someone you trust and who can listen to your plans with your best interests at heart. When thinking about who to talk to, ask yourself how they can help move you forward. Sharing your choices with the right person can help clarify them further and encourage you to go for it.

You may also decide that you need more information in order to make an informed choice. For example, there may be gaps in your knowledge of how many choices you really do have. Where can you find ways to fill these gaps? Do you need to search the internet, read a book, or join a support group?

Give something up in order to gain something of greater value

When we feel stuck and without choices we feel helpless and disempowered. Nobody really wants to get trapped in an unfulfilling job simply because it pays the bills or an unhappy relationship that we are frightened to leave. Given the choice, most of us would say that we would want something better for ourselves. But these can be difficult choices to make. It isn't always easy to see the benefits of giving up the security you believe you depend on. At times, we may feel that we have to sacrifice something we want for something we desire even more. If this is the case, we need to be prepared to let something go in order to gain something of greater value. The root meaning of 'sacrifice' is the same as the word 'sacred'. Viewed from that perspective, we can see our choice as honouring something sacred to us.

Trust your feelings

Trust that you can come up with the appropriate choices to move you forwards. Sometimes you may feel a strong desire to make big changes in order to resolve a situation and move on, and this may be exactly what is required. Other times, it's the smaller choices that you make which are often the most powerful, as well as the most workable. Only you know which choice is the most appropriate. When we think through our options we are using our conscious mind to design strategies and come up with solutions. But it's also important to take into consideration how you're feeling when faced with different choices. Our feelings are powerful indicators of what is important to us and we need to take them into account when choosing one thing over another. When you are faced with a choice, ask yourself what images are associated with the situation and what sensations accompany your thoughts. All your senses can give you clues on a more subconscious level about the options you have and the actions that are right for you.

We so often override our feelings in favour of our more rational side. Learning to trust your senses takes time and practice. Start by simply noticing how you're feeling and you'll gradually start to make connections that help you arrive at answers that come not just from your rational mind, but also from the clues your body gives you. Our bodies speak to us in many ways that we ignore to our detriment. For example, maybe you have a nagging feeling – a gut reaction – that somebody can't be trusted or that a job you've just been offered isn't really right for you. Pay attention to the feeling, it may be a natural apprehension about embarking on a new relationship or taking up a new challenge, or it may be a warning for you to dig a bit deeper and be sure about what you're letting yourself in for.

> learning to trust your senses takes time and practice

brilliant example

Sonia decided to have some coaching because she didn't know which option to choose. She had been married and divorced twice and had had a few short-term relationships in between. She told me that her current boyfriend, who she'd been seeing for a couple of years, had proposed to her and although she felt that she loved him, she was reluctant to get married again. Her ambivalence was tinged with fear that the relationship might end if she didn't commit as her boyfriend wanted marriage and a family. In the coaching process Sonia realised that the prospect of settling down was not the best option for her and even though she felt sad at ending the relationship, she knew it was the right decision. Her desire to be on her own and have time for herself was a more compelling choice.

Think for yourself

Once you have the confidence to trust and believe in yourself, know your own values and what's important to you, you're in a much stronger position to make the best choices. Having your own mind means that you, and only you, decide whether the opinions of others make sense. It means that you don't just accept what everybody tells you or let other people influence you any more than you want to. Having your own mind is about being strong enough to make your own decisions and to stick by them, even if you make mistakes. After all, they're your own mistakes and they can be our greatest learning. It's not about rejecting what people tell you but being able to make your own mind up about what others say and not be afraid to question or even challenge it. That way you are much more likely to arrive at your own sense of what's really right for you.

 brilliant recap

When we learn to trust ourselves and our ability to make the best choices we feel empowered. We honour ourselves when we make healthy choices and this creates a positive context for our lives. Empowering choices have a sense of rightness about them and help us to grow in self-confidence and move forwards in our lives.

 brilliant task for the week

Notice how many choices you make every day and become really aware of what you are choosing. Commit to making the best choices for yourself on a moment-to-moment basis and observe what happens.

CHAPTER 8

Visualise and positively affirm your future

'Every moment of your life is infinitely creative and the universe is endlessly bountiful. Just put forth a clear enough request, and everything your heart desires must come to you.'

Shakti Gawain (b. 1948; author and pioneer in the field of personal growth and consciousness)

D o you believe that your future is already mapped out? Is it written in the stars? Or have you complete free will? Whatever you believe about your capacity to shape the future, the truth is that you have much more choice in how you create it than you might think. This may feel a little daunting, but it's also incredibly exciting. So how exactly do you design your future? How can you achieve your goals and turn your dreams and desires into reality?

Your desire is a powerful force in the creation of your brilliant life. You achieve your desires when you:

- enjoy and appreciate what you already have
- wholeheartedly commit to being the best version of yourself
- take responsibility for your happiness.

Your desire is the catalyst for every life change and your intention determines whether that desire becomes a reality. Your ability to manifest the changes you desire depends on the strength and passion of your beliefs and on the focus of your attention. It also depends on your capacity to imagine and create a vision of your future.

Positive visualisation

When you visualise what you truly want, you make your aspirations more tangible. What was once a wish becomes real and achievable when you create a picture in your mind. The positive mental images that you carry directly influence the quality of your experiences, the way you think and feel about yourself and the outcome of your goals.

There are many ways in which you can consciously manifest your chosen goals. One of them is a process called positive visualisation. A visualisation is an image in your mind of what you want to happen. Positive visualisation is a way of directing your imagination so that you program your subconscious to expect whatever you have just imagined. Positive visualisations instil powerful inner impressions that affect your thoughts, feelings, and beliefs, as well as your outer circumstances. As a result, you feel more positive and empowered and your new mindset begins to attract corresponding circumstances into your life. You are then less likely to be influenced by negative thoughts and experiences, because your thoughts are focused on success and happiness.

> positive visualisations instil powerful inner impressions

brilliant tip

The beginning always takes place in your imagination.

Use your imagination

Remember your imagination is a powerful tool and you can use it to visualise many different future possibilities. Your dreams reflect your cherished wishes and you can translate these into reality with the right mindset. Since dreams have no limitations, feel free to let your imagination explore the landscape of possibilities. The positive energy that this generates will move you into your future. You may think that it's hard to visualise, but this could be a limiting belief. Even if it doesn't come naturally to you, be willing to have a go. Try this short exercise when you are alone and sitting comfortably. Make sure that you won't be disturbed.

 **action**

Simply close your eyes and start to focus on your breathing. Be aware of the steady rhythmic rise and fall of your diaphragm as you gently inhale and exhale. With each breath feel yourself relaxing a little more. Keep focusing on your breathing and let go of any tension that you're feeling in your body. If any thoughts come into your mind, just observe them as passing clouds and go back to your breath. And now imagine yourself in a lovely place, maybe in a beautiful garden or walking along the seashore on a white sandy beach. Visualise yourself as happy and joyful, feeling strong, empowered, decisive and confident. The clearer and more real you can make this vision, the more powerfully you will influence your capacity to be and feel that way. Enjoy being in this place for a few minutes, and when you are ready, bring your attention back to your breathing, slowly bring yourself back into the room and open your eyes.

If you found it difficult to visualise, keep practising until you are able to conjure up an image of a beautiful place in your imagination. When you feel able to do this easily and effortlessly, you can progress to the next step.

Create a 'memory'

Let's imagine that your goal is to run a marathon. Imagine yourself running the race, feeling fit and strong and motivated to reach the finishing line. Feel positive and focus on your visualisation with total commitment and conviction. Keep visualising. Know you can do it. When you mentally rehearse whatever it is that you want to do, you acquire a kind of 'memory' of a successful action and at the same time program your subconscious mind with the outcome you are visualising. If you find it easier to use words, thoughts or sensations you can add these to your visualisation and imbue it with even more energy and power.

Visualise your future self

 **action**

Go back to your circle of life and decide on one area of your life that you would like to project into the future. How would this area of your life look in six months? In one year? In five years?

You're focusing on your ideal life. Visualise it. See it. Feel it. Taste it. Believe in it. You are creating your future in the here and now and making your mental blueprint for your new life. Be creative! Keep picturing your future self in your mind's eye. Allow yourself to experience how you'll feel. See yourself doing the things you'll be doing as your future self. Keep creating mental pictures of what you want. See the incredible future you in the here and now. As you visualise your future self, infuse it with joyful anticipation and feel it becoming a part of you. Let your imagination run wild.

Future me in six months:

....

Future me in one year:

....

Future me in five years:

....

When you visualise your future in this way, it is no longer a place you are going but one you are creating with your imagination, your thoughts and your beliefs. You are breathing life into your future with your creative vision and making it happen in the here and now. Find ways of building positive visualisation into your routine, for example in the bath, in bed before you get up, when you are walking or exercising, on your way to work if you are able to. Live your best life now. Create your happiness now. Know that you are worthy now. And that you will create your best future.

Create a vision board

Another very powerful way to use visualisation is to create a vision board. A vision board is a collage of pictures of the goals and dreams that you want to manifest in your life. You can create your vision board by taking a piece of card, scissors, glue and lots of magazines (or use the internet). Go through the magazines or web search for pictures and images that reflect whatever it is that you want to create. Arrange the pictures on your board in whatever way you feel inspired to do. Enjoy the process of creating a picture of your future life. To give more power to your vision, you can add affirmations to each picture. For example, if you want to create more financial abundance in your life, choose a picture that reflects that abundance for you and write alongside it an affirmation like: 'I enjoy unlimited abundance and prosperity'. This will reinforce your desire. Have your vision board somewhere where you'll see it on a regular basis. Look at your vision board regularly and with focused intent knowing that you are in the process of creating your ideal life and bringing it into reality.

Positive affirmations

Choosing to be optimistic about your future is wonderfully beneficial and essential to the success of your goals. The excitement that comes from optimism changes the way you feel about your-self. Living in vision is one way of staying optimistic. Creating positive affirmations is another.

Positive affirmations are affirming and uplifting statements about yourself and your life that you can say at anytime, either out loud or to yourself. You can repeat your affirmations when you lose heart or motivation, when you need to galvanise yourself or simply to keep you buoyed up. It's important when you say your affirmations to really infuse them with feeling and conviction. Don't just say 'I achieve my goals with ease' in a flat, monotone voice. Say it like you believe it and you really mean it. Savour each word and know the deep truth of your words. Get excited about what you are affirming to yourself.

> really infuse your affirmations with feeling and conviction

Here are a few examples:

- I love and respect myself.
- Every day I affirm my worth and my value.
- I am strong, resourceful and capable.
- I believe in myself.
- Happiness and success are a way of life for me.
- I choose to be optimistic about myself and my life.
- I welcome challenges as opportunities to grow.
- I achieve my goals with ease.
- I am excited about my future.

To help you choose some of your own affirmations, think about a goal you have chosen in the goal setting chapter. Which affirmations would encourage and support you in the pursuit and achievement of your goal? Make a list and display it somewhere easily visible so that you can look at it several times a day.

My goal:

My positive affirmations:

1

2

3

4

5

Constant repetition carries conviction – repeat something often enough and it will start to become you. When you are constantly affirming yourself you are in fact declaring that you deserve to have your dreams come true and that you have the strength of purpose to bring them into being. Don't focus on what you can't do. These are negative affirmations and hold the same power as positive affirmations. Think about what you can do. You have more potential than you know. You can do things you never thought you could do. Most of your limitations are self-imposed. Keep believing in yourself.

 **brilliant** tip

Wholeheartedly repeat something often enough and it will start to become your reality.

The power of optimism

Have you ever heard someone described as having a rather 'Pollyanna' attitude to life? Pollyanna is the story of a young girl whose refusal to think anything negative transformed everyone she came into contact with. In the story, she encourages people to stop seeing themselves as ill, alone or hopeless. Even when life is challenging she teaches them to play the 'glad game', a game where the person tries to find at least one thing to be glad about, no matter what difficulty they are experiencing. In our culture, having a 'Pollyanna' attitude is a term of derision and deemed as being excessively simplistic, cheerful and optimistic, and out of touch with reality. But which – or whose – reality are we referring to? Pessimism makes you feel worse and closes down your sense of what's possible. Optimism makes you feel better and opens you up to life – so which state of mind will you choose?

Expect the best

Adopting a negative or pessimistic attitude never changes anything for the better. It doesn't empower you or enable you to visualise and create a better, brighter future. Quite the opposite. Only the energy of optimism and positive anticipation can help you to create a positive outcome. Choosing to hold a positive expectation is a powerful and potentially life-changing decision. That's because the choice to raise your energy and be optimistic will attract positive experiences to you by the law of attraction. When you believe and act as if you have the power to attract a more loving relationship, a totally fulfilling career or an increased sense of well-being and aliveness, your thoughts act as magnets and attract the best outcomes for you. Being open to your highest good becomes a choice and this informs every thought and action. Your future depends on how you choose to be in the here-and-now. You are creating your future in the present with your thoughts, beliefs and expectations. In fact, the greatest power you can have over your future is the choice to empower yourself now with thoughts and actions that affirm and inspire you. Visualise the best and that's what you will create.

> your thoughts act as magnets and attract the best outcomes for you

 action

Create unstoppable momentum. Visualising your future is a powerful force in the quest for success. Go back to your circle of life and choose one area of life that you would like to positively visualise in the future. Make it a strong intention to create the most vivid, irresistible and exciting picture of your future that you can imagine. Remember that what you think about and focus on the most is what you will create. You'll know your visualisation is working when you can actually feel the physical symptoms of excitement that you would naturally experience in the life that you are imagining. As you answer the questions below, notice which ones inspire and motivate you to make this dream a reality. Keep picturing yourself living your imagined future in all its detail. Keep putting energy into your future vision until you feel like it's already real and in the here-and-now. You don't necessarily need to know right now exactly how it will come about. Maybe all you have is the first step. Allow your mind and your whole being to imagine your future as a fait accompli. Intentionally create new pictures for your future. And use the powerful feelings generated by your visualisation to take action towards creating a world that matches the positive mental pictures and physical sensations of your future life. Keep feeling good about yourself and make this a habit. This will keep you energised and excited about your capacity to create your best life.

Close your eyes and in your imagination, see yourself manifesting your vision:

● How will you feel? Powerful? Joyful? Successful? Ecstatic? Confident? Inspired? Motivated to keep visualising?

● How different will your life be?

● What will change?

● What will others be saying about you?

● What do you say to others about yourself? How does realising your ideal outcome affect your self-esteem and the way that you see yourself?

Is your positive visualisation compelling enough to take the first step towards creating your future self? If so, what action will you take?

Allow yourself to receive

In order to manifest anything in our lives, be it an intimate relationship, doing what you love or better health, you need to be able to *receive* what you want for yourself. This may sound obvious but, in reality, many of us are better at giving than receiving. Often this is the most challenging stage of the process as we uncover or reconnect with any resistance or feelings of unworthiness. In order to be able to receive what you most want, you need to feel good about yourself. When you feel good, you are receptive and magnetic to positive experiences. As you have progressed through the chapters in this book, you have been building your confidence and self-esteem and even if this is still a work in progress, believe that you deserve the very best and trust that this affirmation will work wonders for you.

Keep imagining your wonderful future

Empowering thoughts, the use of affirmations and your imagination are powerful tools for transformation. The more time you spend imagining your successful outcome, the more real and attainable it will feel. When you believe that such things are possible, you have made the first step in making them a reality. Keep visualising your future and planting positive thoughts in your subconscious mind. The exact outcome may not materialise – it could be something even better that you aren't able to imagine at this point in your life. Be flexible and trust that your positive energy and intention will create the best possible outcome.

brilliant recap

Your life is a self-fulfilling prophecy. You create your best future when you visualise yourself as already happy, successful and fulfilled. Keep affirming yourself with positive affirmations and let the power of your imagination conjure up a life of unlimited joy and passion. Never forget that you have the power to create your happiness and success.

brilliant task for the week

Commit to changing one positive affirmation to a deeply held truth. Each time you repeat it, notice the impact it has on your energy and mood.

CHAPTER 9

Create a space for your new life and take the first step

'Man cannot discover new oceans
until he has the courage to lose
sight of the shore.'

Unknown

De-clutter

Once you have clarified your goals you need to clear a space in your life so that you can focus on them and commit to them. The power of de-cluttering cannot be overemphasised and clearing out your home of things that you no longer use or even care for can be a truly transformational process. Even doing a small amount can have remarkable results. When you begin to clear out any clutter in your outside world, it has a corresponding effect on the mental clutter inside you. You may be emotionally attached to your clutter such as an old dress that you love but no longer wear or fit into but you can't quite let go of. Or you may hoard or hold onto things 'just in case' you need them one day. Keeping clutter because you think you might need it someday can drain or deplete your energy. To determine whether something is clutter or not is simple. If it lowers your energy then it is clutter. If you love it and use it, it is not. Even if you are not consciously aware of it, everything in your home has an energetic impact on you.

> if it lowers your energy then it is clutter

 **action**

Explore the energy of your home. Close your eyes and make sure you are sitting comfortably and that you won't be disturbed. Focus on your

▶

breathing and feel yourself becoming more and more relaxed. Let go of any thoughts, simply observing them as passing clouds. Now see yourself walking around your home. Go into each room – what do you notice and how do you feel as you look around you? Does your house feel spacious and light or is it cluttered and a little oppressive? Are there piles of things that are just taking up space? Look in your cupboards and drawers. Pick up different objects and open different cupboards and drawers. Notice what makes your energy go down and what brings it up. When you have done a tour of your home, slowly become aware of yourself sitting in the chair and bring yourself back into the room and open your eyes.

 **example**

Changing the energy

Beth had been given a jewellery box by her mother-in-law before she died. They had never had a good relationship – Beth had always felt judged and undermined by her. Although Beth didn't particularly like the box, she felt duty bound to keep it. Every time Beth looked at the box she subconsciously associated it with feeling criticised, so it subliminally lowered her energy. As soon as Beth realised how negatively the energy of the jewellery box was impacting on her she felt able to give it away. Beth felt an immediate sense of relief and she was delighted that the atmosphere in her bedroom had changed significantly – it felt light and airy for the first time in months.

Make space for the new

Objects have a powerful symbolic value and meaning and clearing things out of your home can have a significant effect on your well-being. Choose one object that you want to clear out and ask yourself:

● What benefit will I have from letting this go?
● What will I lose from letting this go?

● What new things can enter my life as a result of de-cluttering?

For example, if you would like a new relationship but you are holding on to letters and photographs of an old boyfriend, as you clear away these belongings you can positively affirm to yourself: 'I am clearing away the past and opening myself to a wonderful new relationship.'

What's really important

Another way to de-clutter your life and create more energy for you is to determine the difference between vital obligations and non-vital obligations. Vital obligations are things like looking after your children, going to work, paying your bills. Non-vital obligations might be the things you do in the community or for friends. When you are willing to let go of non-vital obligations, you free up your energy and your time for what's really important in your life right now. Think about your vital and non-vital obligations and make a list.

Vital obligations:	Non-vital obligations:
1	1
2	2
3	3
4	4
5	5

Ask for help and learn to delegate

Start by letting go of one or two obligations that negatively impact on your time and energy. In order to do this, you might need to ask for help, delegate responsibility or say no and mean it. Learning to delegate can be a challenge as we like to see ourselves as indispensable or we fear losing control. Asking for help s the load. Experiment by delegating small responsibilities and see how much lighter you feel.

Say no

When we take on too much we can feel resentful. So it's important to be able to say no to the unreasonable demands and expectations of others and of ourselves. When you respect your boundaries and know the difference between vital obligations and non-vital obligations you will be able to say no and mean it. When you feel free to say no and value yourself in this way:

- You feel freer and more energetic.
- You have more time for what's important to you.
- Your self-worth increases.

brilliant tip

Saying no to others is saying yes to yourself.

The two non-vital obligations that I am willing to let go of are:

1

2

Get organised

Taking responsibility for the quality of your life is the biggest shift you can make. Simple lifestyle changes can make a huge difference to whether you have the energy, time and commitment to put your plans into action. Being inspired and motivated is your fuel. But if you're not organised you're not going to get very far. Even the most inspirational dreams will evaporate into the ether if you can't organise your time to nurture them. Start to prioritise and make time for what's really important to you.

 **action**

Try these time-saving ideas:

● Reduce the time you spend on minor or unimportant activities so that you can focus on what you really want to do.

● Only take on as much as you know you can comfortably handle. Learn to delegate.

● Spend less time procrastinating – do it.

● Take control. Make your goals paramount and fit your other priorities around them.

brilliant tip

You always have enough time if you use it wisely. It's a question of priorities.

Discover your priorities

Determining where your priorities lie can be as easy as making two lists; one that outlines all the areas of your life that are vital to your well-being such as 'you time', work, relationships, friendships, exercise, etc., and another that describes everything you do that is not directly related to your well-being, such as watching television, answering e-mails, doing favours for others. This will give you a clear indication of how much time you spend on unnecessary activities that are either stressful or time consuming.

My number-one priorities:	Secondary commitments:
1	1
2	2
3	3
4	4
5	5

When you over-commit or over-extend yourself you can easily burn out. If you do take on too much, ask yourself what the pay off is for overburdening yourself and being so busy. What are the benefits of being more available to others than to yourself? For example, it could be that you like the feeling of being needed or you want to be liked. Having a healthy respect for your time, energy and well-being is essential and your willingness to rebalance your life, no matter how gradually, will enable you to create a truly fulfilling life.

brilliant tip

Is what you're doing getting you closer to your goal? Anything that is wasted effort represents wasted time.

Energy boosters and zappers

Finding out what energises and depletes your energy will have a significant impact on your ability to create your best life. Notice throughout the day what brings your energy up or down and how this makes you feel mentally, emotionally and physically. Some activities and people increase your energy and vitality and others drain and exhaust you. Here are some examples:

Energy boosters	Energy zappers
Going for a walk/run/swim	Doing something you don't enjoy
Ending a hot shower with a splash of cold water	Watching too much TV
Watching the sun rise	Being in a stuffy or artificially lit environment for too long
Repeating positive affirmations	Getting caught up in limiting beliefs

Now write you own list:

My energy zappers are:

1

2

3

4

5

Think of how these activities or thoughts deplete your energy. If you find it difficult to stop doing any of them ask yourself the following questions:

● What purpose does this serve?

● What is the pay-off for this?

● What is it that this allows me to do?

● What excuses do I make for doing it?

Make a commitment to change at least one energy zapper. For example, if your energy is depleted by being around someone who is negative or critical of you, make a conscious decision to spend less time with them or avoid them altogether. Commit to having more joy in your life.

Now consider what boosts your energy.

My energy boosters are:

1

2

3

4

5

See if there are any other ways in which you can increase or expand these in your life on a daily basis. Enjoy the benefits of doing what uplifts you.

 **example**

Superwoman

Sophie was a super mum. She worked full-time, was on several committees and spent a lot of time fundraising and doing things in the community. She was juggling too much and every area of her life was suffering as a result. She knew something had to give but she didn't know what.

In her life coaching sessions she discovered that she felt incredibly guilty and anxious at the prospect of giving anything up. She thought that people might judge her for being selfish and that she'd lose respect and even friends. She also realised that she had sacrificed the things in her life that she used to love like being in nature and making pottery. Sophie came to a painful but liberating realisation that she was making the admiration that she got from others for being a super mum more important than her own happiness and well-being. She also realised that it was easier to devote herself to others than to give herself the same love and attention. She worked on her self-worth and gradually began to let go of the obligations that depleted her and started doing the things that made her feel good about herself.

Sophie learnt to value herself and her own needs and create goals that enabled her to develop in new ways. She's still very busy but she now feels fulfilled and energised and her life is much more balanced.

Find time for you

Changing your life takes time and energy. So it's important that you remember to replenish yourself. When you take on too much and try to fit a long list of activities into every minute of the day, you become depleted. Recharge your batteries by finding time to focus on taking care of yourself. 'You time' is essential if you are to function at your best and create balance in your life. If you think that it's selfish to focus on your needs, think again. Balancing your needs with the needs of others honours both you and them. Become self-centred. This simply means that you are in tune with yourself, prioritising your own well-being and taking care of the most important person in your life – you. Everyone benefits when you choose to take the very best care of yourself because you have energy available for all aspects of your life.

> 'you time' is essential if you are to function at your best

Recognising the importance of 'you time' is one thing. Finding a place for it in your busy lifestyle can be more of a challenge. To make the most of 'you time', make sure that you don't squeeze it in between hectic activities. Consider how you would most love to spend your time and forget for a moment the demands of your everyday life. You may discover that you are inspired to do something creative, become more physical or just simply be. 'You time' gives you the space to reflect on your life and equips you to instigate the changes you want to make.

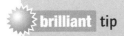

brilliant tip

'Self-centred' is being grounded and focused.

 example

Making space for a new life

Joel had left a high-powered job in the City after a series of minor health problems. He knew he was burnt out and needed some time out to reassess his life and make some much needed changes. During his first life coaching session he focused on his circle of life and was shocked to see how low he had scored each area. He'd put all of his energy into work and his life had become completely unbalanced to the point of exhaustion.

After a couple of sessions it emerged that Joel was passionate and very knowledgeable about flowers and plants and that what he would really love to do was start his own planting business. He felt excited and energised at the prospect of doing something he loved, even though he recognised that he needed to slow down for a while. He focused on building enough self-belief to launch his own business and used his positive visualisation and affirmations to inspire and motivate him. Once he'd set his goals he created a plan of action. He also created a timeframe and gave himself a year to be up and running.

In the meantime, Joel created some time and space in life. He took a part-time job for a few months at his local bookshop and spent a lot of his free time reading gardening books and learning more about his subject.

Joel opened for business right on schedule and he has gone from strength to strength. He is doing what he loves and as a result his business is thriving.

Take the first step

There are times when your life is pointing you in a new direction. When a new path reveals itself you have several choices. You can ignore it, consider it but agonise over whether to do anything about it, or discover where it's leading to. Even if you are unsure at first, taking this first step leads to another step that will take you where you need to go. New directions open up when it is time to make a life change. Once you decide to move forward and you focus on your goal, you've started the momentum for change and you are already half way to achieving it. Your ability to embrace a bigger life depends on your willingness to keep moving into new spaces. Each step you take into the unknown strengthens your resolve to keep expanding your possibilities.

> new directions open up when it is time to make a life change

There are many paths that open in the course of our lives, leading us into relationships, jobs, friendships and previously unknown aspects of ourselves. Your life up to this point is the result of all the paths you have chosen to explore, and your continued growth depends on your ongoing curiosity to discover more about yourself. Taking the first step can be an exhilarating moment. You have stepped across the threshold into a new life.

Pluck up the courage to begin

There's only one way to start to change your life for the better. And that's to start. And as the first step is often the hardest, you will need a specific goal to work towards. Remember to take one step at a time towards your goal. Decide which goal feels most important, even if it may be a little risky. Primarily your goal needs to be congruent with who you really are. It may even reflect a change in your values. For example, you may be moving from valuing putting others' needs first to putting your own needs first. When you do that, you are more willing to go after what you want and your goal will reflect this. Travel light and don't burden yourself with negative thinking. Your positive energy will keep you on track. Keep visualising the goal you want to reach and the next steps will become apparent. Think of your success as the sum total of small efforts repeated on a daily basis.

Listen to your intuition – your inner knowledge always knows which step you need to take next.

 **brilliant** tip

It's the job you never start that takes the longest to finish.

Take your time

Every big achievement is made up of little accomplishments. Change is an evolutionary process and takes time. If you want to grow an apple, you need to give it time to blossom, bear fruit and then ripen. A caterpillar doesn't metamorphose into a butterfly overnight; it spends a period of time in the chrysalis before it emerges and takes flight. We also have our own timetable for change. Think of your goal as a seed and your role is to provide it with the optimum conditions in which to come to fruition. Be patient and keep visualising the outcome.

Trust the process

There's a time for pushing forwards and a time for holding back. Sometimes you just need to hold the vision of your new life and wait for something to unfold. This can be a very creative time as the seeds you have sown begin to take root and grow. But it requires trust as it may appear that nothing is happening. The times that you find yourself in limbo can be used to reflect on where you are and how you are feeling. You may discover that you need to be more proactive in some way. Ask yourself if there is anything else you could be doing to move things along and take action. If no action is required on your part, review the situation in a few days' time and enjoy the in-between time, knowing that your future awaits you.

 **tip**

Lying fallow is a time of renewal as you imperceptibly evolve into the new you.

Personal power

What does personal power mean? Many of us falsely believe that it means exerting our will over others. But the true definition of personal power is having a clear sense of your own strength, self-worth, resources, skills and abilities. Personal power allows you to make your own life a priority and know that you are worthy and deserving of the very best. When you are in touch with your personal power you act decisively and know that your goals are within your reach. You discover that you can do what you were afraid you couldn't do. And you commit to being all of who you can be.

> commit to being all of who you can be

What makes you feel strong and in your power?

● Knowing how you want your life to be.

● Committing to taking action to create your best life.

● Being authentic – choosing thoughts and beliefs that uphold the truth of you.

Add your own ideas to the list below.

I am strong and in my power when I:

1

2

3

4

5

Do what makes you feel strong and empowered and you will be unstoppable.

brilliant recap

When you decide to commit to your new life you will inevitably need to make some changes. You may need to let go of certain things as well as non-vital obligations that prevent you from focusing on your own life. Learn to prioritise and create 'you time'. The more you invest in yourself the more energy you will have for your life.

brilliant task for the week

Commit to letting go of one non-vital obligation and use the time that is freed up for you.

CHAPTER 10

How to stay motivated

'Your destiny isn't a matter of
chance, it's a matter of choice.
It's not something you wait for,
but rather something you achieve
with effort. Never give up on your
dreams. You *do* have the power to
make them a reality.'

Patanjali (2nd century BC; founder
of Yoga sutras)

Knowing what you want is one thing. Having – and keeping – the motivation to make it happen is another. The Buddhists talk about living life as if your hair were on fire. In other words, when something is important enough you make it a number one priority and all of your energy goes in that direction. Your motivation needs to feel like a burning desire if you truly want success. When you're motivated, you draw on all of your resources, rally all of your faculties, marshal all of your energy, and focus your heart and your mind on attaining your objective. You're 100 per cent committed to yourself and your aspirations, and your thoughts and your actions support your commitment.

What motivates you?

However inspired you are by your goal, there are times when your energy can start to flag. When this happens, you need to plug yourself back into the source of what motivates you and use motivational tools to get you back on track. Here are some motivational tools.

Know your worth

Although our sense of self changes as we journey through life, we tend to measure our worth by how much we've accomplished, how intelligent, good looking, prosperous or talented we think we are. The opinions of others can often dictate how we feel about ourselves. The truth is that your inherent worth has nothing to do with these factors. Your true worth is innate and can't be eradicated by anyone or anything and once you value yourself for who you are your life begins to change from the inside out. Every time you affirm yourself and treat yourself with respect you grow in self-confidence and self-esteem. When

> once you value yourself for who you are your life begins to change

you feel worthy you have no problem accepting yourself as you are. It is your self-worth that enables you to feel happy, confident and motivated to become the best you can be.

Keep your creative juices flowing

When you're thinking creatively you are open to new insights and perspectives. You literally pluck ideas out of thin air. Your creative juices flow and you feel buzzing and alive and you bring enthusiasm and energy to whatever you're doing.

🏃 brilliant action

Here are some suggestions to keep your creative juices flowing and your motivation high.

- Check in with yourself and ask yourself such questions as 'What makes me excited about my goal?' and 'Why do I want to achieve it?' Have a pad of paper and write whatever comes into your head. Be inspired by your answers.

- Seek inspiration – read books and see films about people who have done extraordinary things with their lives or succeeded against all the odds.

- Dance, sing, exercise, meditate – any of these change your mental and physical state.

- Breathe deeply for five minutes, oxygenate your lungs and empty them of stale air. You'll feel revitalised as every cell in your body is replenished.

● Drink more water. When you're dehydrated you lose energy and vitality. Without proper hydration your brain – which is 85 per cent water – can't do its job properly and you can't function at your best.

Adopt an attitude of gratitude

It's easy to lose sight of the positives in your life when you direct your thoughts towards what isn't working in your life. Focusing on the negatives and what's missing depletes your energy and isn't conducive to attracting what you want. It creates a feeling of dissatisfaction and a belief in lack, and this then becomes a self-fulfilling prophecy. When you focus on what you are grateful for and have an attitude of gratitude, you create a feeling of abundance and this helps generate more of what you want.

Write a list of five things that you appreciate and are grateful for in your life right now. Can you think of any more?

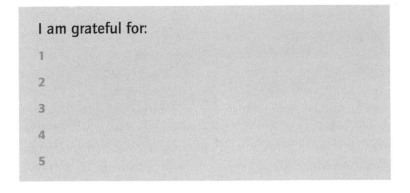

I am grateful for:

1

2

3

4

5

Mentally go through your list when you wake up in the morning and go to bed at night. Think about what you are thankful for in every aspect of your life. Let your gratitude be heartfelt. Even a situation that you wouldn't normally think of as something to be grateful for could be seen as a blessing with hindsight. Remembering all of the good things that you already have is a very powerful way of raising your energy and staying motivated.

Raise your vibration

We all know how it feels to be vibrant. Vibrant literally means 'pulsing or throbbing with energy'. In fact everything is made of energy. Different forms of energy vibrate at different speeds. Human beings also vibrate at different energetic frequencies and your thoughts and feelings can determine the frequency at which you vibrate. When you think negative thoughts you deplete your energy and you lose power. Think positive thoughts about yourself and your future and you literally increase your vibrancy. Keep your motivation strong by raising your vibration.

think positive thoughts and you literally increase your vibrancy

Fine-tune your goals – change direction if your goal no longer inspires you

A lot can change along your journey and you may decide you want to move the goalposts or even change your goal. If your goal no longer sets you alight you will need to find out what has changed. The most important criterion is whether the underlying value of your goal is still true. For instance, if your goal is to meet a partner within six months but half way through the process you recognise that it would be more beneficial for you to keep focusing on your own development, your value has changed and therefore your original goal no longer resonates with you. In order to keep your motivation strong it's important to review your goals from time to time to make sure that you are still congruent with them. Ask yourself whether you and your goals are still a perfect match. Fine-tuning your goals gets you back on track and gives you the means to move forward.

 **tip**

Success is the sum of small efforts, repeated day in day out.

 **example**

Choosing what's right for you

Belinda had decided that she would continue with her career for one more year and then start a family. She loved her job as an editor of a glossy magazine and had worked hard to get to the top. However, she felt her biological clock was ticking and she was afraid that if she didn't get pregnant soon, it would be too late. Six months later Belinda was asked whether she would be interested in becoming the editor of a brand new magazine. She immediately felt a rush of excitement at the prospect of such a challenge. Every fibre of her being wanted to say yes to the offer but in doing so she knew she would have to postpone getting pregnant.

After one coaching session Belinda became really clear that taking the job was the right decision for her. She knew that at 32 she could afford to wait a while longer before switching priorities. She decided to take the job and set a new goal – to re-evaluate her life in two years' time.

One step at a time

So often we want to reach our destination without experiencing the journey. We can run out of patience or even hope if it takes longer than we anticipate to reach our goal. Each step of the way is a potentially valuable experience if you choose to see it that way. Everyone who has succeeded in reaching their goal did this by taking the first step and then adding a second, third and so on until they reached their destination. Trust that each step is taking you closer to your goal and your motivation will stay strong.

Reward yourself

Rewarding yourself can be a very good way of staying buoyant. Giving yourself a reward is a way of acknowledging how well you are doing. Just make sure that your rewards are congruent with your goals. For example, if your goal is to eat more healthily and lose 4 kilos in one month, rewarding yourself with a big bar of chocolate when you lose your first kilo may be counterproductive! Reward yourself in such a way that you feel inspired to realise your goal – treat yourself to a weekend at a spa or become a member of a health club.

Be accountable

Accountability is when you don't want to let yourself (or anyone else) down. It means that you take full responsibility for what you have said you were going to do. That doesn't mean that your goals are written in stone. But it does mean that you make an agreement with yourself to follow through to the best of your ability.

Be flexible

Focusing all of your energy on one specific goal is very effective, but it's important to bear in mind that there can be more than one outcome. Remain open to other possibilities because there just might be one that you hadn't considered.

Get energised

Keep moving your body. When you do physical activity it moves your energy, clears your head and raises your spirits. Do whatever you enjoy – dancing, walking, an exercise class, swimming and do it often.

Get enough rest

We all have days that seem difficult and hard. On these days, it is as if the odds are stacked against us and one challenge follows another. This is part of the process. If you feel stuck it may be a sign that you need to recharge your batteries. When your energy is flagging the solution can be as simple as getting a good night's sleep. When you're rested you feel ready for the day and whatever it will bring. If you are still feeling daunted, making a small change in your perception can have a dramatic effect on how you are feeling. Perhaps you've always told yourself that you need at least eight hours' sleep and that you can't function on less. Experiment with that belief and see whether it's really true. You might surprise yourself.

when you're rested you feel ready for the day

brilliant tip

Every experience can be transformed into something of value. It all depends on your perspective.

Focus on the present

Our past can often feel like a burden. If you feel as if you're carrying something that is undermining your ability to move forwards, commit to letting it go. This can take time and you may need help, so be gentle and patient with yourself and get support if you feel that you need it.

Find your own motivational strategies

Keeping your motivation alive takes energy and commitment. Add your own motivational tools to the list below. Make them a part of your life, a part of how you approach each day.

● Keep affirming your belief in yourself and in your ability to achieve your goal. State you affirmations in the present tense: 'I am capable and confident.' 'I have a fabulous career.' 'I'm in a loving relationship.'

● Keep affirming that you deserve the very best. Remember that you receive what you believe.

- Keep visualising the outcome you intend and really feel the excitement of this reality. This is a powerful way to energise your goals.

- Stay open to unexpected developments. You can transform every challenge into an opportunity with the right mindset.

- Be patient and trust the timing of your life changes. Everything comes to fruition at the right time.

 **tip**

Enjoy the journey and expect the best.

 **example**

Trust in the process

There's a well-known story about a man who was observing a butterfly in the process of emerging from the chrysalis. After what seemed an eternity of watching the butterfly struggling to get free, the man decided to help it along. He took a penknife and cut open the chrysalis and the butterfly fell out. The man waited expectantly for the butterfly to flap its wings, but to his dismay he realised that the butterfly was unable to fly. The energy and effort it takes to break out of the chrysalis is what strengthens the butterfly's wings. Without that challenge the butterfly can never reach its full potential.

Ask the right questions

When you're excited about a goal, you live it and feel it as a reality. You're motivated to accomplish it and you feel uplifted every time you think of it. However, the excitement – and the resulting momentum – can be blocked if you feel conflicted. You may feel energised about a certain goal, but you may also experience other things such as fear, worry or anxiety. For example, you may want to lose weight, but you may also dread the exercise and sense of deprivation that you expect to experience before accomplishing your desired results. You may long to fall in love but worry about feeling vulnerable again. Or want a career change but feel a sense of hopelessness about your prospects.

Often the questions underpinning these doubts are:

● What if I fail?

● What if I'm not good enough?

● What if I succeed?

When you uncover these questions you can immediately reframe them to:

● What is the best way for me to succeed?

● How can I put my many skills and abilities to good use?

● How can I enjoy my success?

Keep affirming a positive perception of yourself and believe that you're capable of manifesting your goal. If you desire a new relationship this means believing in your capacity to love and be loved. If you desire greater financial rewards, this means believing you deserve to be abundant.

brilliant tip

Whatever you believe or feel about yourself will inevitably attract the same in return.

Get support if you need it

Even with the best will in the world we can still sometimes succumb to our inner saboteur. Just when we're doing really well on our healthy regime, we stop exercising or taking vitamins, even though we feel better when we do. Sometimes we catch ourselves in the act of self-sabotage, especially the more that we work on ourselves, but it can still happen unconsciously, which is why it can be difficult to see that we are doing it. Simply recognising that you are doing something that is undermining your ability to achieve your goal can dispel its power. If further effort is required, get help from one of your support team.

get help from one of
your support team

Go beyond your expectations

When you adopt a positive perspective your thoughts motivate you to go beyond what you previously thought possible. Keep pushing the boundaries and feel excited about the *terra incognita* that you are about to discover.

brilliant tip

The more inspired you are the greater is your potential to actualise your best self.

Choose a role model

Your motivation to create a new life is your most powerful incentive. Finding a role model who embodies everything that you admire can inspire you in your quest to be the best you can be. This person could be a fictional character or a real person, perhaps someone you know personally. Focus on what attracts you to them and what you most admire about them. It may be their courage and determination or their visionary qualities which have made such a big difference in the world. Can you recognise any of

finding a role model can
inspire you to be the
best you can be

these qualities in yourself? We often project the parts of ourselves that are less developed or that we are not aware of onto others.

List the qualities that you most admire about your role model.

The qualities I admire in my role model are:

1

2

3

4

5

The qualities I share with my role model are:

1

2

3

4

5

 **brilliant** recap

Motivation fires you up and propels you forwards towards your goals. Using all or just a few of the motivational tools available to you keeps you energised and focused and excited about the life you are creating.

brilliant task for the week

Choose two of your motivational tools and apply them to your life on a daily basis. Keep a record of how they impact on your energy and focus.

CHAPTER 11

Enjoy your journey

'Expect the best; convert problems into opportunities; be dissatisfied with the status quo. Focus on where you want to go, instead of where you are coming from; and most importantly, decide to be happy knowing it is an attitude, a habit gained from daily practice.'

Denis Waitley (b. 1924; author, keynote lecturer and productivity consultant)

Greater fulfilment

Congratulations! You've embarked on a journey of transformation and chosen to commit to your best life. You've taken the challenge of finding out who you really are and what you truly desire for yourself. This is no mean feat and inevitably involves a few bumpy moments. When life is difficult, challenging or uncomfortable we are unlikely to feel good about what is happening. But life can still be fulfilling even when we are learning some painful lessons or having to push ourselves far out of our comfort zone. It is possible to be struggling with change and uncertainty and still have a sense of rightness and even calm about what is happening. There are even times when we need to do something that doesn't feel good in order to experience greater fulfilment, such as leaving an unhappy but financially secure relationship, or a stressful but highly paid job.

 **brilliant** tip

Fulfilment is the full expression of who we are.

Happily ever after

In fairy tales the hero and heroine only get to live happily ever after once they have reached their goal. We have an expectation that we will only awaken with a kiss or be happy when we have accomplished a particular task. In actual fact, we can live happily even as we go through the dark forest alone or fight our dragons. If you are creating a life around your values and what you know is right for you, you have the vital ingredients for enjoying your journey even when the going gets tough.

When the going gets tough

So you're moving in the direction of your dreams and you recognise that the journey can be challenging at times. These challenges can sometimes present as setbacks – maybe you applied for a job, got to the final three in the selection process and weren't chosen, or the relationship that you've been working so hard at falls apart. At times like these it's easy to feel like a failure. Don't even go there. There's a big difference between failing at something and being a failure. You are never a failure even if something doesn't work out. When something doesn't go according to plan ask yourself:

> challenges can sometimes present as setbacks

- What do I really want?
- Why do I want it?
- Do I believe I really deserve it?

These questions will help you to regroup and discover what else you can do to bring your dreams to fruition.

Think of a situation in your life where you didn't succeed in the way that you'd hoped. What did you learn from the situation? Did something good come out of it?

See the gift

You can reframe your challenges by making it a daily practice to spend some time before going to bed each night acknowledging the gifts and opportunities that you received that day.

This transforms your perception of what you might ordinarily see as a bad day. Some days it's easy to recognise the gifts you've received; on other days you have to look harder, but once you do you will find there are always one or two. Seeing the positive in what appears to be negative doesn't always feel authentic at first. Trust the give and take of life and remember that sometimes the best gifts are the ones that we don't recognise straight away.

 **action**

Think about where you are in your journey. What are the gifts that you are being given? Make a list and keep adding to the list on a daily basis.

brilliant tip

Appreciate the gifts as you are advancing along the path of your goals and purpose.

The value of challenges

When you make your purpose in life to grow into the best human being you can be your ability to be happy no longer hinges on finding the right partner, becoming successful or even making a valuable contribution to society. You become more accepting of the fact that your life doesn't have to be perfect and things don't always go smoothly. We are supposed to experience challenges and it is precisely those challenges which enable us to grow into our full potential. Think about the incredible trans-formation of a piece of coal into a diamond. This doesn't just happen. The earth applies pressure to the piece of rock, heats it and exposes it to exactly the right conditions to turn it into a beautiful, sparkling diamond. Think of yourself as a diamond in the making and embrace the challenges that enable you to grow into your most precious self.

Growth is not always comfortable. It can be scary and painful letting go of where you were in your life and moving in a new direction. But that doesn't mean that something bad is happening. Have you ever gone through a challenging time and looked back and said 'I grew so much – it was the best thing that ever happened to me?' At the time you probably didn't see it that way because it didn't feel good. How could something beneficial be happening if you felt miserable? But we can learn to see the value of our challenging experiences whilst we are in the midst of them. We can be present and recognise that what is happening has a purpose and is for our highest good. You can enjoy your journey of transformation by constantly reminding yourself of this truth and finding the courage to keep growing as you move towards your goals. It will make you feel good.

growth is not always comfortable

Rather than judging yourself on how perfectly you are fitting into a picture of how you think your life *should* be progressing, start to evaluate yourself and your journey through life by how much you are growing and how fulfilling that process is for you. When you do that your happiness no longer depends on achieving your goals but becomes an intrinsic part of how you live your life.

brilliant tip

Embrace the challenges that life presents you, and challenge yourself often.

▶ brilliant example

Be happy in the now

Kate didn't feel good about her life. She had recently gone through a painful break-up and had put on nearly a stone in weight. Not only that, but her small business was floundering. She felt a failure and her self-esteem was rock bottom. Her faith in life had been shaken and she felt that nothing was turning out the way she had expected it to. Before Kate and her partner parted company, she believed that the purpose of her life was to get married and create a highly successful business. She had worked all hours to try to get her business up and running and as a consequence the time she and her partner spent together had been limited. Kate admitted that she hadn't ever really enjoyed her life but she had been holding on to a 'happily ever after' scenario in her head and that was her *raison d'être*. She had sacrificed being happy in the here and now.

In her life coaching sessions Kate came to the realisation that much of her life was driven by what she thought she 'should' do and as a result she hadn't ever felt fulfilled. She felt inspired to stretch herself by rethinking her career and spending some time getting to know herself and what made her happy.

You can enjoy your journey on a daily basis if you:

● are grateful for your life and the opportunity to learn and grow

● are kind to yourself even if you have a bad day

● learn one thing about yourself

● don't indulge in an old negative thinking pattern and instead choose one that makes you feel good about yourself.

☀ brilliant tip

Look for happiness, focus on happiness and you will create happiness.

More navigational tips to help you enjoy your transformational journey

Release your endorphins

No matter what is happening in your life, create a space for fun and joy in your day. Dance or sing along to some of your favourite music. Share a heartfelt exchange with a friend, colleague or even a stranger. Lift your spirits by laughing more. Laughter releases endorphins, the body's feel-good chemicals, and boosts your immune system. You take in a lot more oxygen when you're laughing and that also increases your elation. Go to comedy clubs, see funny films and spend time with people who share the same sense of humour with you. Connect with your inner child and become more playful. You also release endorphins when you exercise, relax and make love – which is why these activities are so beneficial.

connect with your inner child

> ☼ **brilliant** tip
>
> Enjoying the journey means focusing on what fulfils and inspires you.

Say yes to life

From the moment you wake up, choose to say yes to your life. Whatever the day brings can be seen as a blessing if you accept what is happening in the here and now. You can't always choose your experiences but you can choose your reaction to them. When you do that you feel in control of your life and how you experience it. And you achieve self-mastery. Don't make yourself miserable by resisting what is. Say yes and make any changes you need to from a place of acceptance. You'll enjoy your life so much more.

Live your life as a special occasion

Have you got a particular outfit that you love but rarely wear, or maybe some beautiful cut glass crystal glasses that are hidden away for months on end? Are you saving these things for special occasions? Change your perspective and see your *life* as a special occasion. Live your best life now by wearing your most fabulous clothes and enjoying your most treasured possessions.

Have quality time

The healthier and more balanced we are, the better we function. No matter how busy or demanding your life is, make room for quality time and engage in joyful and energising activities that feed your mind, body and spirit. When was the last time you bought yourself some flowers or did something special just for you? Remind yourself of how special you are. Cook yourself something delicious, lay the table as if you were expecting an honoured guest and enjoy a candlelit supper with the person you love and nurture the most – you.

> remind yourself of how special you are

Lighten up

Do you know why angels have wings? It's because they take themselves lightly. Take yourself lightly and smile. Learn to laugh at yourself. You don't have to take yourself so seriously. You can only do your best. You don't need to strive for perfection. Take the stress and struggle out of your journey by reminding yourself to lighten up.

 **brilliant** recap

Never lose sight of the fact that becoming your best you is an eventful and exciting journey. Enjoying the journey is a gift that you can give yourself. You don't need to wait until you have reached your target weight, met your ideal partner, started your own business or have more money in the bank before you can be happy with your life. You can enjoy your journey of transformation in the here and now. Remember that happiness is a state of mind. Ask yourself 'How can I experience more joy in my life?' and see what your subconscious comes up with. When you know that you deserve to be happy you can make the most of each moment and congratulate yourself on having committed to your best new life.

Remember that the beliefs, thoughts, affirmations and visualisations that you have in the present are creating your reality – now and in the future. So be mindful of this moment, live it and enjoy it. Be glad to be alive.

brilliant task for the week

Make a commitment to yourself to incorporate at least two navigational tips into your daily routine. Notice how these impact on your ability to enjoy your life.

CHAPTER 12

Congratulate yourself on reaching your destination

'Life is no brief candle for me. It is a sort of splendid torch which I have got hold of for a moment, and I want to make it burn as brightly as possible before handing it on to future generations.'

George Bernard Shaw (1856–1950; playwright, dramatist and literary critic)

You've come a long way and you've been on an illuminating journey in the pursuit of your goal. In the process you have burned brighter, grown stronger, wiser and more resilient and discovered resources and talents that you never knew you had. You've learned that if you want to change your life you need to change the way you think and question what you believe. You've found a different perspective on your life and specific ways to grow in self-belief, self-confidence and self-worth. You've challenged yourself to go beyond your comfort zone and change your self-defeating patterns into self-empowering ones. You've moved beyond the limits that you previously set and opened up to new perspectives.

You've accepted that your life is not about being perfect but about doing and being the best you can. You've woken up to the fact that everything you need to be happy is within you and that you create your own reality moment by moment. You've decided what it is that you truly want and you've set goals and achieved some if not all of them. You've expanded your vision of what is possible, of who you are and what you are. You've connected with an experience of your best self.

You've said 'yes' to yourself and to doing something different. And in so doing, something else has taken over which is your willingness to take risks, increase your level of trust and belief in yourself. And you've recognised the importance of looking after you and creating a more balanced life in which you always honour and nurture yourself. Perhaps surprisingly to you, you've begun to see the ripple effect of the changes you have made. The way you are changing your life and how you are responding to life's experiences may have inspired others and motivated them to expand their horizons and possibilities.

You've begun to experience first-hand the fact that others benefit from your choice to make your well-being paramount. Not just because you have more energy to devote to others but because when you do what you love and live according to your own truth, you inspire others to do the same. Most of all you have embraced your life and committed to living your purpose as joyfully as you know how. You've become your own brilliant life coach!

Recommit to yourself

It's a wonderful feeling when you attain your goals and these are times in your life to savour and celebrate. Give yourself credit and acknowledge what you have achieved. Not just the big goals that you set for yourself, but all the small steps along the way and everything that you have become in the process. Thank the people that have supported and championed you. You may feel that you wouldn't have got to where you are without them, but never underestimate the fact that it was your drive, your vision, your curiosity, your self-belief and your willingness to grow and learn that made it happen.

give yourself credit and acknowledge what you have achieved

So where do you go from here? Life is always changing and there will be new adventures and challenges to experience. But there are some things that can become a constant in your life and that will act as a compass, always guiding you to the truth of who you are. It's easy to forget who we are, how powerful we are and what we can create with our beliefs and intentions. So we need to remind ourselves – on a daily basis. Recommit to living a life based on joy and growth instead of struggle and fear. Begin your day with this intention and let it be your guiding principle. Recommit to:

● being curious and finding a different way of thinking if the old way doesn't work

● stepping out of your comfort zone every time you feel in danger of becoming bored or stuck and seeing this as a wake up call

● taking action based on your intuition and trusting what feels right to you (aka leaps of faith)

● exploring new pathways when they appear before your eyes

● living your life to the full

● challenging your beliefs and assumptions and being willing to think out of the box

● becoming the very best you can be.

This is the greatest gift that you can give to yourself, and as the famous TV ad says, 'You're worth it.'

Keep creating your best life. You've discovered that it is possible – that you can do it – and it's not just an option for people who are more talented, deserving, capable and clever than you thought you were. You've tapped into the energetic law of magnetic attraction – that you attract whatever you radiate and what you focus on expands. And last but not least, you've discovered that the most important relationship that you will ever have is with yourself. Your life will never be the same again.

> your life will never be the same again

 brilliant tip

See your life as an ongoing journey and fully commit to the long haul.

9780273714804

9780273743217

9780273730675

9780273743231

9780273720591

9780273717355

9780273725-14

9780273721239

9780273712350

Whatever your level, we'll get you to the next one.
It's all about you. Get ready to shine!